Opting Out of Digital Media

Opting Out of Digital Media showcases the role of human agency and cultural identity in the development and use of digital technologies. Based on academic research, news and trade reports, popular culture and 105 in-depth interviews, this book explores the contemporary "opting out" trend. It focuses directly on people's intentions and the many reasons why they engage with or reject digital technologies. Author Bonnie Brennen illustrates the nuanced thinking and numerous reasons why people choose to use some new technologies and reject others. Some interviewees opt out of digital technologies because of their ethical, political, environmental, religious or cultural beliefs. Other people consider new media superficial diversions that do not meet their expectations, needs or interests, while some citizens worry about issues of privacy and security and reject digital technologies because of their fears. Still other people construct their cultural identities through the choices they make about their use of new media. In many cases, the use or nonuse of digital technologies offers specific representations of how people assert their independence, authority and agency over new media, while in some cases the choices that people make about new technologies also illustrate their class position or socioeconomic status.

Opting Out of Digital Media responds to the growing opting out trend, addressing the developments in the unplugging phenomenon. It serves as the ideal text for any reader interested in the role of digital technologies in our lives and how it has become a part of a mainstream movement.

Bonnie Brennen is Professor Emerita at Marquette University and editor-in-chief of *Journalism Practice*. Her research addresses relationships between media, culture, technology and society. She is the author/editor of seven books and one novel and her research has been published in edited books and academic journals.

Disruptions: Studies in Digital Journalism
Series editor: Bob Franklin

Disruptions refers to the radical changes provoked by the affordances of digital technologies that occur at a pace and on a scale that disrupts settled understandings and traditional ways of creating value, interacting and communicating both socially and professionally. The consequences for digital journalism involve far-reaching changes to business models, professional practices, roles, ethics, products and even challenges to the accepted definitions and understandings of journalism. For Digital Journalism Studies, the field of academic inquiry which explores and examines digital journalism, disruption results in paradigmatic and tectonic shifts in scholarly concerns. It prompts reconsideration of research methods, theoretical analyses and responses (oppositional and consensual) to such changes, which have been described as being akin to "a moment of mind blowing uncertainty".

Routledge's new book series, *Disruptions: Studies in Digital Journalism*, seeks to capture, examine and analyse these moments of exciting and explosive professional and scholarly innovation which characterize developments in the day-to-day practice of journalism in an age of digital media, and which are articulated in the newly emerging academic discipline of Digital Journalism Studies.

Journalism Between the State and the Market
Helle Sjøvaag

Opting Out of Digital Media
Bonnie Brennen

Photojournalism Disrupted
Helen Caple

For more information, please visit: https://www.routledge.com/Disruptions/book-series/DISRUPTDIGJOUR

Opting Out of Digital Media

Bonnie Brennen

Routledge
Taylor & Francis Group

LONDON AND NEW YORK

First published 2019 by Routledge

2 Park Square, Milton Park, Abingdon, Oxon OX14 4RN
605 Third Avenue, New York, NY 10017

*Routledge is an imprint of the Taylor & Francis Group, an informa
business*

First issued in paperback 2022

British Library Cataloguing-in-Publication Data
A catalogue record for this book is available from the British Library

Library of Congress Cataloging-in-Publication Data
Names: Brennen, Bonnie, author.
Title: Opting out of digital media / Bonnie Brennen.
Description: London; New York: Routledge, 2019. |
Series: Disruptions: studies in digital journalism |
Includes bibliographical references.
Identifiers: LCCN 2019009324 | ISBN 9781138601734
(hardback: alk. paper) | ISBN 9780429469947 (ebook)
Subjects: LCSH: Digital media—Social aspects. | Choice (Psychology) |
Digital media—Psychological aspects.
Classification: LCC HM851 .B7355 2019 | DDC 302.23/1—dc23
LC record available at https://lccn.loc.gov/2019009324

ISBN: 978-1-138-60173-4 (hbk)
ISBN: 978-1-03-233836-1 (pbk)
DOI: 10.4324/9780429469947

Typeset in Times New Roman
by codeMantra

Contents

1 Getting started

Opting out trends

On July 27, 2018, I came upon a display of board games and puzzles at my local Target store in Haverhill, Massachusetts, with the heading: "Unplug and Play." As a ubiquitous brick and mortar U.S. retailer, second only to Wal-Mart, I wondered if the Target sign was just a play on the term plug-and-play device or if it was actually a sign that the opting out movement had successfully gone mainstream.

During the last few years, there has been a growing trend questioning the role of digital technologies in our lives. Public calls to resist digital culture's shiny objects and to unplug, slow down, restrict and/or opt out of new media have become more urgent, sustained and popular. Contemporary researchers are finding people increasingly frustrated and overwhelmed by the constant intrusions of digital devices into their lives. They suggest that smartphones keep us in an extended state of anxiety where we feel the need to constantly touch them, check them and respond to them. Researchers are now recommending that people need to step away from their phones and take breaks from their use of digital media. Technology leaders are cautioning that the development of Artificial Intelligence (A.I.) may have catastrophic results for humanity. Facebook has acknowledged that too much social media takes us away from face-to-face social engagement and that it can be harmful to our mental health. Facebook's acknowledgment of its impact on society, in response to shifting public perceptions of the role of social media and following reports of Facebook spreading propaganda and disinformation during the 2016 U.S. presidential election, now seems particularly significant.

Digital detox retreats, vacations and programs, designed to help break Internet addictions, have become increasingly popular and habit-breaking mobile apps are being developed to help people overcome their digital technology habits. In addition, a growing digital temperance movement is focused on helping individuals take back control of their use of new technology. This book responds to the growing opting out trend; it addresses developments in the unplugging phenomenon and offers evidence to support a determination that in the U.S., unplugging from digital technologies has become a mainstream movement now affecting millions of Americans.

When I began this study in 2015, the opting out movement was limited and was often characterized in the popular press as a fringe activity. Initially, there was limited coverage in mainstream media and popular culture, but during the last three years, the amount of coverage has significantly grown. Opting out has become a regular topic addressed in major news publications and magazines. There are now frequent first-person accounts, opinion columns and news reports, surveys and scholarly research about individuals and communities opting out as well as opportunities for digital detoxes and guidance for individuals interested in managing their new media use. A quick look at the reference section of this book illustrates the diversity of recent opting out coverage.

Although the level of digital inclusion continues to increase and has become less dependent on education, income, race, location, age and/or gender, a recent study by the Pew Research Center suggests that about 30 million people in the U.S. do not use email or the Internet at all. While some of these individuals find it too expensive, too difficult or too frightening to use, many other people reject digital technologies because they do not find them relevant, interesting or integral to their lives. Approximately, one-third of nonusers or about 10 million adult Americans are actively choosing not to engage with digital technologies at all because they are not interested and consider them irrelevant to their lives (Anderson, Perrin and Jiang 2018). In addition, a growing body of research suggests that many millions of other Americans are taking an active role in deciding which technologies they engage with and which ones they choose not to use.

During my research for this book, I discovered that a significant number of people intentionally use new technologies with specific social purposes, practices and needs in mind. Responding to the growing research and public commentary on this issue, this book draws on contemporary academic research, news reports and elements of popular culture that address the ways individuals are actively making decisions about their use or nonuse of new technology. It also incorporates insights from 105 in-depth semi-structured qualitative interviews that I conducted with individuals who self-identified as having strong views about their technology usage.

My interviews took place from 2015 to 2018 with an ethnically, culturally and geographically diverse group of Americans. Fifty-nine people self-identified as white, 11 as multiracial, 13 as black or African American, 12 as Asian, 9 as Hispanic or Latina and 1 as an American Indian. I personally interviewed 53 men and 52 women, whose ages, at the time I spoke with them, ranged from 20 to 81. Fifty-three interviewees were in their 20s and 30s, 27 were in their 40s and 25 interviewees were 50 years of age or older. Twenty interviewees were undergraduate or graduate students, 13 were retirees, 12 referred to themselves as "stay at home moms" and 60 interviewees were employed full time.

The interviews lasted from 45 minutes to two and a half hours and were held in homes, offices, coffee shops, over Skype and on the telephone. I interviewed 55 people in person, 11 over Skype and I conducted 39 interviews on the telephone. While all of my interviews were with U.S. citizens, recent research has indicated that opting out was more than an American phenomenon. Therefore, where possible, this book incorporated global insights and examples to augment U.S.-based surveys, interviews and other research. Ultimately, I was interested in understanding the specific reasons why some people chose not to engage with new technologies and how individuals made decisions about the technologies with which they interacted.

I discovered that apart from a consistent preference to read books on paper, there were a multitude of reasons why individuals used some technologies and rejected others. Some people opted out because of their ethical, political, religious or cultural beliefs. Others found new technologies simple diversions that did not meet their needs or interests and by opting out, they took back their time and refocused their lives on family and community concerns. Some people worried about issues of privacy and security, rejecting new technologies out of safety concerns, while others asserted their independence, authority and dominance over technologies as they constructed their individual identities through the choices they made regarding their use of digital technologies.

The diversity of option about why the interviewees opted in and opted out of digital technologies began with their conceptualizations and definitions of what constituted new media. When I asked interviewees how they defined digital technology, their responses ranged from "all mobile-based technologies," "everything using screens," "all digital technologies," "smartphones," "social media – especially Twitter and Facebook," "everything online," "recent technologies that are better than the older ones" to "just about everything new that's not alive." Other interviewees used a cutoff date to define new technologies such as "every technology created since 2010," "technologies introduced in the last two years" and "digital technologies developed in the twenty-first century."

This project began with research published in the *Routledge Handbook of Developments in Journalism Studies* edited by Scott Eldridge and Bob Franklin. Like this book, the original research was framed by Raymond Williams' theory of cultural materialism, which restores human agency and intention to the development of new technologies and maintains that people create and use new technologies with specific needs, interests and practices in mind. While some key themes were identified in my earlier work, for this book I was able to conduct additional interviews and expand my research to include much greater depth of analysis of recent trends, topics, issues, themes and concerns.

The remainder of this chapter addresses contemporary research and conceptual foundations that are particularly significant for understanding the opting out movement. It addresses contemporary research on the digital divide and the technology resistance movement and outlines conceptual foundations that frame the existing research and guide this book project.

Chapter 2 describes the many facets of the digital temperance movement and the variety of events and efforts that encourage people to control their use of digital technologies. This chapter outlines the creation of the Sabbath Manifesto and discusses the development of technology-free zones, digital detox programs, retreats, vacations and camps along with community efforts to limit children's access and use of new media.

Chapter 3 tackles the development of A.I., machine learning and algorithms, and discusses the fears and concerns raised by researchers, ethicists and technology experts regarding these new media. This chapter also addresses A.I. fears raised in news reports and in popular movies as well as the concerns raised by the people I interviewed.

Chapter 4 discusses the contemporary trend of mixing analog technologies with digital media usage. This chapter focuses on the use of paper books, magazines and newspapers, typewriters, pens, film-based cameras and record albums commonly referred to as vinyl and it considers the ways people integrate some of these older technologies with newer digital tools in order to develop their cultural identities.

Chapter 5 focuses on how cultural, political, ethical, environmental and religious values influence individuals' use and nonuse of digital technologies. This chapter also considers how some interviewees utilize digital technology to manage their productivity and control the influence of new media on their lives.

Chapter 6 describes privacy and security concerns connected with digital listening devices that track people's movements and actions and record their conversations. This chapter also discusses privacy risks connected with surveillance activities, online banking and the disclosure of personal information.

Chapter 7 addresses security issues and privacy concerns related to social media and discusses why some people choose not to engage with any social media. This chapter also considers the role of human agency in interviewees' decisions about social media and illustrates ways people develop their personal identities through their relationships with Twitter, Facebook and other social media.

Finally, Chapter 8 showcases socioeconomic and class issues that influence the relationships people have with new media. This chapter also considers the influence of digital technologies on interviewees' construction of their cultural identities identifying some ways interviewees assert their dominance and independence over new technologies and provides some additional commentary on the opting out trend.

The digital divide

Considerable research about the use of digital technologies has been framed around the dichotomy of the haves versus the have-nots. Known by politicians, public leaders, journalists and researchers as the digital divide, this approach envisioned the haves as individuals who acquired a variety of technological resources to help them live well. In contrast, the have-nots were people assumed to live in unstable environments without the resources to purchase new technologies. Maintaining that people who were left behind in the digital revolution would never rise above the underclass, researchers considered nonusers digitally deprived, insisting that the use of new technologies was a critical component for the development of a strong socioeconomic foundation. Mack (2001) explained:

> While computers and the Internet are certainly no panacea for all of society's ills, these technology resources assist people in developing and improving their skills, knowledge, marketability and income. Ironically, those who could most benefit from these resources are often foreclosed from acquiring or accessing them.
>
> (p. 42)

Early digital divide researchers assumed that access to new technologies was a fundamental resource necessary for success in contemporary democratic societies. Believing that no right-minded person would voluntarily reject the use of new technologies, digital divide researchers primarily investigated the conditions, issues and problems restricting individuals' access to new technologies. Hindman (2000) clearly explained digital divide researchers' basic assumption when he wrote: "In an era of digital convergence, nonuse and nonaccess to information technologies may lead to perceived nonexistence" (p. 549). In an attempt to determine which issues were responsible for creating and maintaining the digital divide, researchers have focused on key characteristics, including age, class, race, gender, ethnicity, socioeconomic status, education, geography, household type and marital status.

As rates of digital inclusion continued to grow, some researchers began to question the continued relevance, basis or existence of a digital divide. For example, Harambam, Aupers and Houtman (2013) noted that a basic assumption of the digital divide research was "not only that all people *should* make use of the internet, but also that everyone actually *wants* to do so" (p. 1108). They maintained that contemporary digital divide research failed to consider the agency of nonusers, who were actively making decisions about their digital use and nonuse. For Harambam, Aupers and Houtman, it was important for researchers to go beyond an emphasis on structural inequalities to consider the cultural and social processes that were foundational for the consumption and use of new technologies (p. 1109). In contrast, Sparks (2013) has suggested the relevance of a digital divide perspective continued because the concept has been equated with social, economic and political inclusion and since its inception, it has had "a normative bias towards the benefits of digital inclusion" (p. 30).

Throughout its history, digital divide research has primarily been framed from a technological determinist perspective, which maintained that our growth from an industrial society to an information society reflected the development of new technologies, which were directly responsible for creating modern people, societies and cultures. Embracing a prevailing perspective on the role of technology in social change, technological determinists have envisioned new technologies as changing our social relationships and institutions in order to create the necessary conditions for the development of our modern world. The creation of new technologies has been viewed as either a self-acting force that resulted in a new culture or society or as a self-acting force that produced materials necessary to construct a new way of life (Williams 1974/1992). From this vantage point, it was assumed that technologies have fundamentally altered modern societies and therefore people should have full access to new technologies and must embrace those technologies, so that they can fully function in the modern world.

In his assessment of digital divide research, Gunkel (2003) found that the existing research assumed that digital technology effected "socioeconomic opportunity and success" (p. 511) and reduced socioeconomic problems to technological challenges. This technology-centered perspective did not consider how the uses of technology were shaped socially and culturally nor did it consider human agency and the reasons why people used or rejected new technologies. Similarly, Wyatt, Thomas and Terranova (2002) have questioned framing research on the use of new technologies from a technological determinist perspective because it "confirms the technocratic vision of the centrality and normativity of technology" (p. 25).

Cultural materialism

This book rejected the perspective of technological determinism and instead drew on the theoretical framework of cultural materialism, which focused directly on human intention and agency and maintained that individuals developed and used new technologies with certain social needs, purposes and practices in mind. Although technological determinism has pervaded much of the research on the incorporation of digital technologies, cultural theorist Raymond Williams (1974/1992) found technological determinism an "untenable notion" because it substituted the random autonomy of intention or "an abstract human essence" for individuals' "real social, political and economic intention" (p. 124). In contrast, Williams insisted that new communication technologies have been created and developed by individuals who had specific "purposes and practices already in mind" (p. 8). Williams (1977/1988) offered his concept of cultural materialism, which was a theory of the "specificities of material cultural and literary production within historical materialism" (p. 5), as a viable alternative to technological determinism. The centrality of culture, as the lived texture of each social order, was a fundamental component of cultural materialism, which according to Williams privileged experience while combining an emphasis on both creative and historical agency.

Specifically, from a cultural materialist theoretical framework, people were seen as active agents whose individual experiences helped to create their own culture (Williams 1977/1988). Ultimately, this theoretical framework restored human intention and agency to the research and development of new technologies. Addressing the specific development and production of elements of material culture within its particular historical context, cultural materialism shifted the emphasis, privileging human experience as a fundamental component of all cultural analyses.

While none of the 105 interviewees explicitly said that their socioeconomic status or financial concerns influenced their use or nonuse of digital technologies, it emerged during their conversations that class and economic issues related to some of their decisions. Many interviewees addressed cultural, social, religious and political factors that affected their decisions regarding their use of new media as well as the processes they used to help them make informed choices about their engagement and nonengagement with digital technologies.

Opting out research

Although the digital divide has figured prominently in research on the incorporation of new media, some scholars have also considered individuals' deliberate choices regarding their use and nonuse of digital technologies (see for example, Rauch 2014 and Wyatt 2003). Most of this research has framed the lack of engagement with new technologies as a problem or pathology or as acts of resistance, refusal or pushback against the "evertime" (Morrison and Gomez 2014) of constant connectivity.

Because social science researchers generally considered the use of digital technologies appropriate, expected and normal, when they investigated people who rejected new media, their work has tended to frame opting out as a weakness, a concern or a problem. For example, Murthy and Mani (2013) found that people rejected digital technology because it was too complex, too expensive, not flexible enough or because nonusers had technology fatigue with ever-changing products and excessive choices. Unwilling to consider that some people might not find digital technologies interesting, useful or relevant to their lives, for Murthy and Mani, if developers fixed the problems they identified, no one would ever want to opt out of new media in the future.

The terms that social scientists have used to describe nonusers also illustrated their assumption that opting out was a problem that needed to be dealt with quickly. Researchers have referred to individuals who previously used digital technologies but gave them up as "cyberspace dropouts" (Katz and Aspden 1998), "Internet dropouts" (Rice and Katz 2003), "Internet defectors" (Kingsley and Anderson 1998) and social networking "quitters forever" and "quitters for a while" (Dindar and Akbulut 2014). In addition, Stieger, Burger, Bohn and Voracek (2013) investigated the "phenomenon of virtual identity suicide" (p. 629), which was the term they used to describe individuals who stopped using social media like Twitter or Facebook, while Karppi (2011) referred to the process of opting out of social media as "digital suicide."

In contrast to social scientists who have considered the lack of engagement with digital technologies a concern that must be fixed, some humanist researchers have rejected technological determinist assumptions that have framed much of the nonuser social science studies in favor of research that granted agency to those who chose to opt out. Rather than seeing opting out as a symptom of apathy, laziness or as a pathology, some researchers have recently framed opting out as a conscious act of resistance. While the introduction and use of new technologies has been thoroughly studied, according to Foot (2014), until recently the vast majority of nonuse studies have focused on digital divide issues and concerns. Foot dated the rise of digital technology resistance research to between 2009 and 2011, when concerns about social media intensified in the political, military, organizational and personal spheres. Using the term "pushback" to mean reducing or rejecting media use, Foot also included "altering media practices, and attempting to influence media policies" (p. 1315) as components of the media resistance movement.

Portwood-Stacer (2012) chose the term "media refusal" to refer to the actions of individuals who did not use Facebook and suggested it was through a focused revolt of "conspicuous non-consumption" (p. 1047) of Facebook and other elements of consumer culture that individuals created their own identities and remade their lives into sites of media resistance. Similarly, Woodstock (2014) used the expression "media resister" to represent a person's purposeful, thoughtful and active rejection of digital technologies. Considering media resistance a complicated and sometimes contradictory act, Woodstock suggested:

> As active, elective makers of meaning, media resisters may ignore particular types of media content (such as news or popular culture), or they may refuse to adopt one new media technology but not others. And like most of us, they are not necessarily consistent.
>
> (p. 1987)

In contrast, Kuntsman and Miyake (2016) maintained that the growing "digital dis-engagement" trend that encouraged resistance, refusal and pushback from new technologies included paradoxical practices like posting selfies of unplugging from social media or blogging about unplugging. Finding that some resisters used various devices, tools and technologies to promote their opting out practices, Kuntsman and Miyake (2016) questioned the authenticity of new media resistance and asked: "can digital disengagement even be possible as long as it relies on those same digital tools?" (p. 14). Responding to the potential paradox of unplugging from the ubiquity of digital technologies, Hesselberth (2017) appeared to answer Kuntsman and Miyake's question by maintaining that the value of media resistance was in helping citizens to renegotiate the contemporary "culture of connectivity" by weakening the "hold that the logic of mass-mediated connectivity has on us" (p. 14).

While media resistance research may at first glance seem to be based on Williams's theory of cultural materialism because the research restored human intention to decisions regarding individuals' use of digital technologies, it is important not to assume that all resistance research rejected a technological deterministic conceptual framework. A major theme of the digital disengagement research has focused on individuals' fears regarding the influence or effects of technology. Some media resistance research may actually be what Williams (1974/1992) has called a "peculiar doomsday brand of technological determinism" (p. xvii) because it assumed that changes in societies have been entirely based on the introduction and development of new technologies. Not all individuals' experiences showcased in the resistance research have been based on individuals who made their own decisions; instead, some of the actions have been the result of people reacting to the perceived power of the technology to change their lives. The digital disengagement literature certainly has illustrated ways people resisted new technologies, but it might also be seen to limit our understandings of all of the varied reasons that people chose which technologies they engaged with and which technologies they rejected.

For example, a recent study analyzing commentary on media refusal found in blogs, popular press and academic research by Morrison and Gomez (2014) suggested a five-part typology that described individuals' motivations for resisting digital technologies. The first part was emotional dissatisfaction with the technologies, which focused on individuals who had high expectations regarding new media but who later became disillusioned, bitter or even angry with digital technologies because they did not meet their needs. The second part involved the rejection of new media because of people's religious, moral or political beliefs. The third aspect of the typology showcased limiting the use of digital technologies in order to save time and energy, while the fourth part involved pushback against new technologies because people were fearful that they would become addicted to them. The final part of the typology focused on fears about online technologies particularly related to ways that individuals' privacy was being violated.

Identity creation

While there were many instances that the experiences of the people I interviewed related to Morrison and Gomez's typology, I found that much of the interviewees' commentary was not clearly ranked or differentiated. In addition, the majority of the 105 people who I interviewed highlighted an additional motivational theme – identity creation. Throughout this book, interviewees explained that their incorporation or rejection of new technologies was an important way that they created their own identities. Opting out was a key way that they actively showcased the issues and concerns that were central to them, and their views toward digital technologies illustrated the role of new media in each of their lives. Rather than viewing their actions solely as acts of resistance to technologies that were exerting power over them, many of these people saw their actions as asserting their independence, authority and dominance over the technology. Throughout this book, a variety of perspectives on opting out are addressed; while some views fit well with the existing technology resistance literature, many other experiences do not illustrate any type of resistance but instead showcase aspects of identity formation.

This book draws on Stuart Hall's (2000) conception of cultural identities, which envisions identity as being composed of a variety of open-ended, shifting, fragmented and sometimes "contradictory" identifications. These identifications are historically, not biologically, situated and are based on race, class, gender, sexuality, ethnicity and nationality as well as from an individual's personal and public experiences. Hall's view counters the belief that an individual's personal identity is biologically constructed and remains fully formed and consistent throughout that person's life. Cultural identity also differs from a classical sociological view that identity is created from a person's interaction with him/herself and other significant members of society. Instead, for Hall there is no one permanent identity. Individuals have different identities at different times and some of these contradictory identifications will lead them in very different directions.

As Hall explains, identity is a "movable feast: formed and transformed continuously in relation to the ways we are represented or addressed in the cultural systems that surround us" (Hall 2000, p. 598). In other words, there is no one overarching identification that determines a person's identity. An individual's social class, race, sexuality and political orientation may create contradictory identities that can change and transform a person's cultural identity.

In addition, it is through the development of identity formation that opting out may be seen to challenge a class-based socioeconomic foundation of digital divide research and its key assumption that many people who do not use digital media are information-deprived because they cannot afford new technologies that are necessary to fully participate in democratic societies. A key finding of this research is that these days more people are choosing not to engage with digital technologies because they can afford not to do so. As Hesselberth (2017) recently explained, within our contemporary "culture of connectivity," the digital divide may actually be "an indicator or class, educational, and/or gender privilege" (p. 6).

Based on recent research and my interviews, I discovered that some nonusers of digital technology were members of the intellectual or economic elite; if they desired, they were financially able to delegate technology-related tasks to others. These individuals did not need to engage with social media or perform Google searches, send and/or receive emails or texts because they had others who could complete such tasks. They did not need to purchase tablets or iPads to entertain their children while they worked, because when they could not be with them, their children were being educated or entertained by tutors, sitters and/or nannies. When they were able to spend time with their children, they were able to give their children their full attention. The economic or intellectual elite attended digital retreats and vacations, in part because they had plenty of vacation time. They had no major problems going off the grid because they had a network of employees and support persons who were able to cover for them or because they made going off the grid a cultural or intellectual priority. Ultimately, in contemporary American society, as the level of digital inclusion has dramatically increased, many individuals who opted out actually did so because they could afford not to have to live in an "evertime" of connectivity.

2 Digital temperance movement

There has been an exponential growth in the Internet of Things, which is the networking of vehicles, appliances and other devices in order to communicate and exchange information online. This enormous network of connected devices can be monitored or controlled remotely, and it influences our personal relationships and our interactions with everyday technologies. People throughout the world are concerned that the line between our online and offline lives has become increasingly blurred. They worry about the development of the Internet of Things and the intrusions of digital technologies on their lives and their concerns are fueling a digital temperance movement.

Uneasy about the development of an online life that often "breeds narcissism, alienation and depression," (Douthat 2017) a multifaceted movement is focusing on helping people take control of digital technologies to restore balance to their lives. According to Bartlett (2018), currently there is "a palpable demand for anything that involves less tech, a fetish for back-to-basics." The digital temperance movement is not an anti-technology campaign but rather an effort to consider the impact of new media on our lives. Some members of the temperance movement look to France for guidance, because it is currently leading efforts to restore a work/family life balance. In 2017, France passed the right to disconnect legislation, which gave employees the right to disconnect from digital technologies after work and on weekends.

This chapter focuses on the digital temperance movement, addressing social and cultural efforts to help people take control of their use of new technologies. It explores the creation of the Sabbath Manifesto and the rise of technology-free zones, digital detox retreats, vacations, programs and camps that encourage people to unplug. It also discusses community efforts to limit children's use of digital technologies. Taken together, the topics in this chapter offer a way to understand a diverse but increasingly common phenomenon.

Technology-free zones

For more than 30 years, Sherry Turkle, the Abby Rockefeller Mauzé Professor of the Social Studies of Science and Technology at the Massachusetts Institute of Technology, has been studying the psychological aspects of online connectivity. Turkle's research suggests that digital technologies not only change what people do, but they also impact the type of individuals that people become. While she does not advocate giving up our mobile devices, she stresses the need to use them with "greater intention." Turkle recommends that people take time away from digital media in order to communicate face-to-face with others and she suggests: "We can carve out spaces at home or work that are device-free sacred spaces for the paired virtues of conversation and solitude" (Turkle 2015, p. 6).

Technology-free zones, where Internet use is discouraged or even forbidden, is thought to help individuals restrict and control their digital technology usage. Signs such as "The use of WMDs (wireless mobile devices) is not permitted," "This is a screen-free zone," "Talk to me – not the screen" and "There is no app to replace your lap! Read to your child" are regularly seen outside businesses, coffee shops and restaurants. Some local restaurants in London offer discounts of up to 25 percent to patrons willing to lock up their phones during their meals, and restaurants in Europe and the U.S. offer discounts and incentives to encourage diners to put away their screens during meals. Locally owned franchises of Chick-Fil-A restaurants throughout the U.S. have offered customers free ice cream to put their devices away while they eat and McDonalds restaurants in Singapore offer mobile phone lockers to encourage their diners to have real conversations during their meals. While a few cafes in the U.S. have banned cell phones completely, a growing number of restaurants encourage technology-free meals by providing diners with tableside decorative boxes in which they can store their cell phones (Ballentine 2018).

Physicians have become increasingly concerned about the effects of constant connectivity on our physical and mental health. According to a 2017 Vision Watch Survey, overexposure to digital technologies has resulted in an increase in digital eye strain. With millions of people using smartphones each day, individuals are frequently reporting eye strain symptoms, including dry eyes, headache, blurred vision and neck or shoulder pain. A recent survey by the American Psychological Association (APA; 2017), on the relationship between social media, other digital technologies and health and well-being, found that the continuous use of new media has become a significant source of stress for adults. About half of the Millennials surveyed worried about the influence of social media on their mental and physical health, while almost half of parents surveyed were concerned about the pervasiveness of social media on their children's physical and mental health.

Sixty-five percent of Americans surveyed by the APA noted the importance of managing digital technologies and indicated that they were controlling their family's technology usage by limiting screen time and periodically unplugging. About 20 percent of those surveyed indicated that they did not allow cell phones or other devices during meals or during time spent with family members and friends.

Thirty-five of the people I interviewed spoke of putting their cell phones away during meals so that they could spend quality time with friends and family. For example, Destiny,[1] a 25-year-old marketing manager from Philadelphia, Pennsylvania, said that she tried to balance her digital technology use when she was not at work:

> When my friends and I get together for dinner and drinks we always put our phones away so that we can spend time together without distractions. We have a rule that the first one who grabs their phone has to pay.

Similarly, Marcus, a 37-year-old contractor from Michigan, said that he left his smartphone at home when he went out with friends because:

> you know, you can't have real conversations with people when you're constantly staring at your phone. The first time I went out without my phone I kept checking my pocket for it but you know, now I feel my connections are deeper when I'm without my phone.

Television program plotlines are beginning to address technology-free zones. For example, *The Affair* (2018), a drama on the premium cable TV network Showtime, recently showcased a wealthy family going device-free during meals. The eighth episode of season four featured a scene where two of the main characters were directed by their hostess to put their cell phones in a basket before lunch because "meals are for human interaction." Also, the reality television series *Unplugged Nation*, shown on the FYI network in the U.S., focused entirely on living off the grid. Hosted by unplugged lifestyle expert Jay Gruen, who guided families on unplugging, the participants learned about self-sufficiency and becoming more environmentally conscious about their housing decisions.

Businesses have been showcasing concerns regarding constant connectivity through the development of workshops and lectures. Each year CAMP brings together 200 innovators for a four-day mix of business, creative arts and movement workshops in the mountains of Big Bear, California. Emphasizing community, discovery and learning, CAMP was completely screen free and participants have been required to relinquish all their devices at check-in (theuniquecamp.com). In addition, digital detox strategies have been showcased at International Spa Association expos and bridal planners have found that many couples currently preferred device-free weddings where cellphones were strictly prohibited at the ceremony and guests were asked not to upload photographs to social media. Wedding photographers frequently mentioned that when guests were able to use digital technologies at weddings it was difficult for them to take good pictures because so many guests spent their time looking down at their phones (Bilton 2014b). Unplugging has even become a popular advertising strategy for businesses. For example, the 2017 #UnplugForMom campaign, by the diamond jewelry store Zales, encouraged Americans to put down their digital technologies and interact face-to-face with their moms on Mother's Day.

Technology executives at places like Twitter, Tumblr, *Huffington Post* (now HuffPost) and Yahoo have recommended regular unplugging to help people balance their virtual and real lives (Bilton 2013). Arianna Huffington, current CEO of Thrive Global and former editor in chief of *The Huffington Post*, regularly turned off her cell phone so that she could think and reconnect as did Davie Hayes, head of creative strategy for Tumblr, and Chris Moody, Chief of Data at Twitter (Mawad and Rahn 2015). Former Facebook executive Randi Zuckerberg encouraged people to unplug in order to understand how best to use digital technologies to create a healthy balance between their virtual and real lives. Zuckerberg suggested that when people unplugged, "we respect our personal time, we value our loved ones and we control our devices, not the other way around" (quoted in Clark 2015).

Apps to unplug

As discussed in Chapter 1, researchers like Kuntsman and Miyake (2016) have found the notion of unplugging paradoxical because people regularly used digital technologies to help them step away from other new media. But the struggle to manage digital technology usage is real, and media firms have responded to the seemingly addictive nature of their products by developing a variety of tools and apps designed to help individuals manage their technology usage.

In an effort to reduce vibrations, lights, rings or other disruptions, Apple's Do Not Disturb feature for its iPhone, iPad and iPod touch devices offers users the option to silence calls, notifications and alerts. Users may also set their devices to only receive calls from specific people or to alert them if someone calls repeatedly. In addition, Apple's iOS 12 operating system for the iPhone and iPad comes with Screen Time, which is a tool to help users manage the time they spend on their apps and devices. Users are encouraged to set time limits for categories of apps like games or social networking sites or they can establish time limits for individual apps. Once the time limits have been set, "when you run out of time with an app, it locks you out" (Chen 2018).

Other apps such as Mute, Space and Moment have also been designed to help people manage their technology use. Mute tracks smartphone use and logs users "detox streaks," while Moment sets limits to cell phone usage much like Apple's Screen Time. The Space app begins with a quiz to help determine each user's phone type and then it encourages that person to change his/her phone habits by setting unplugging goals (Dredge 2018). Thrive is a bidirectional app offered by Arianna Huffington in partnership with Samsung. In an effort to help it users manage their screen time, Thrive blocks incoming calls, messages and notifications and also sends text messages to inform individuals trying to reach the users that they are currently unavailable (Fowler 2018a). Some apps have gone even further to help people limit their technology use. For example, Digital Detach implements a timed detox that turns off all smartphone functions except making telephone calls and texting, while the Digital Detox app turns off every mobile device feature except dialing 911 in an emergency (Borchers 2015).

Sabbath Manifesto

Created by Reboot, a group of writers, artists, filmmakers and media professionals focused on affirming Jewish traditions, rituals and cultural values – the Sabbath Manifesto – which provides a blueprint to help people slow down and unplug from technology. Offering concrete tools to push back against the increasing demands on our time and energy, the manifesto explains: "Way back when, God said, 'On the seventh day thou shalt rest.' The meaning behind it was simple: Take a break. Call a timeout. Find some balance. Recharge." The Sabbath Manifesto offers ten core principles to help people slow down and reconnect with others in order to make their lives more meaningful. These principles should be observed each Sabbath: (1) avoid technology; (2) connect with loved ones; (3) nurture your health; (4) get outside; (5) avoid commerce; (6) light candles; (7) drink wine; (8) eat bread; (9) find silence; and (10) give back (available at www.sabbath.manifesto.org).

People are encouraged to engage with the principles of the Sabbath Manifesto in order to determine how best to find balance in their lives. To some individuals, "give back" might involve volunteering at a homeless shelter while for others it means donating to their favorite charity. Some people interpret "avoid technology" as recommending that they do not check social media while to others it means not using any digital media. The Manifesto calls for a weekly 24-hour Sabbath break that encourages participants to unplug, give back to their communities and reconnect with their families and friends. Each week, Reboot sends a Friday afternoon email with creative suggestions on how participants can spend the digital Sabbath (Irvine 2012).

Emmy-nominated filmmaker Tiffany Shlain and her family have observed a digital Sabbath for several years, which she found helped them to spend quality time together and allowed her the time to think more creatively about her filmmaking (Cattel 2015). Founding partner of the Australian firm Productivity Training Daniel Sih has also observed a weekly Digital Sabbath in order to enjoy the benefits of technologies without becoming reliant on them. Sih turns off all digital technologies for 24 hours and does not use the Internet, watch television or check his social media accounts, to do lists or calendar. While he has found unplugging challenging, Sih maintained that "the benefits are enormous. By disconnecting from technology, I find that I reconnect with life. I reconnect with my wife and 3 kids. I reconnect with friends (not on Facebook). I reconnect with God, with nature and with myself" (Sih 2014). Journalist Andrew Sullivan (2016), a self-described early adopter of "living-in-the-web," has written about individuals taking a digital Sabbath as a way to help them rebalance their lives. Sullivan first decided to unplug after he realized that "Every hour I spent online was not spent in the physical world. Every minute I was engrossed in a virtual interaction I was not involved in a human encounter."

During my interview with Shayna, a 40-year-old book editor from Philadelphia, Pennsylvania, she said that she has participated in a digital Sabbath each week for the past five years. At sundown each Friday night, Shayna's two children turned off every digital device in the house and the family sat down together for dinner. "It's a great time to catch-up with each other and have a meaningful conversation."

Whenever possible, on Saturdays the family went outside and explored their neighborhood. They have also held Scrabble tournaments, played cards and listened to music. Shayna said that both she and her husband used digital technologies throughout the day at work, but that by the end of the week she often felt "distracted and exhausted by all of the technology. Since we've been celebrating Digital Sabbath my husband and I both seem to have more energy. Unplugging helps me to unwind and relax and enjoy the weekend with my family." An outgrowth of the Sabbath Manifesto is the National Day of Unplugging, which has been held each March since 2010. It is intended as a time to power down, self-reflect and reconnect with family and friends. According to Rabbi Danny Gottlieb, "In these days, when technology is a constant in our lives, the opportunity to shut it all down for a day is a rare and precious gift" (quoted in Bartlett 2015). Gottlieb suggested that the National Day of Unplugging was an opportunity for people to engage in face-to-face conversations and spend quality time outside enjoying the beauty of nature. The National Day of Unplugging is currently a worldwide event and people from more than 125 countries with varied backgrounds and religious affiliations participate.

Digital detox

As a start-up technology executive, Levi Felix worked extremely long hours until he became ill and was hospitalized in 2009 for exhaustion. Felix began to reevaluate his priorities; he quit his job and decided to travel throughout Asia with his girlfriend Brooke Dean. During their journey, they had limited telephone or Internet access for extended periods, but by the time they returned to the U.S., Felix was determined to spread the word that people needed to unplug. In 2012, Felix explained: "I love that technology connects us and is taking our civilization to the next level, but we have to learn how to use it, and not have it use us" (quoted in Mele 2017). Unfortunately, Felix's concerns now seem strangely prophetic in that he died in January 2017 from a brain tumor at the age of 32.

Felix and Dean cofounded a retreat from technology called Digital Detox and offered a mission statement known as the Digital Detox Manifesto, which was based on an overarching belief in "living a life of freedom, balance and joy." Valuing human interaction that was balanced with thoughtful engagement with nature, the movement respected "the power of play, mindfulness, integrity, intention, spontaneity, self-expression, audacity, creativity, community, authenticity and vulnerability." According to the Manifesto, the role of technologies should be to:

> serve as tools to connect us to these tenants as we celebrate life, truly improving our unique existence, instead of distracting, disturbing or disrupting us. And we believe that these technologies should be created mindfully and ethically, for the benefit of and not at the cost of consumers and users.
>
> (available at digitaldetox.org)

Unplugged programs, camps and vacations

In 2013, Digital Detox began to sponsor Camp Grounded, an all-inclusive technology-free adult summer camp. First held in Northern California, then expanded to include camps in New York and Texas, the camp sessions have addressed the role of digital technology in people's lives. All participants were required to give up their electronic devices, which were placed in plastic bags labeled "biohazard" (Mele 2017). Felix noted that people rarely understood how they used digital technologies "as a social crutch – as a way to avoid anxiety or loneliness" (quoted in Petrow 2015). At the camps, people meditated, read, swam, hiked, cooked, participated in talent shows, talked and interacted with others. News blogger Matt Haber attended a three-day Camp Grounded session and found that without digital distractions he was able to connect more fully with others while learning some important insights about himself. Haber described what he envisioned was the goal of Camp Grounded: "By removing the things that supposedly 'connect' us in this wireless, oversharing, humble-bragging age, the founders of Digital Detox hoped to build real connections that run deeper than following one another on Twitter or 'liking' someone's photo on Instagram" (Haber 2013).

While completing a digital detox may be tempting to some people, Health.com found that many of its readers were unable to completely unplug from digital technology even for a day. In response, the magazine published a three-week digital detox challenge for its readers in the June 2017 issue of Health.com. The goal of the challenge was not to unplug completely but to help people get more control over their technology use in order to enjoy their lives and become "fully present to themselves and to other people" (Andriakos 2017). Week one began by creating technology-free zones to help people disconnect at specific times. Readers were advised not to access their smartphones for the first 30 minutes of each day in order to establish screen-free routines. The challenge recommended readers go screen free during meals (at least dinner) and encouraged them to set boundaries for their technology usage. Week two focused on breaking the bond with digital devices by turning off alerts, creating technology-free entertainment each day and encouraging those participating in the challenge to embrace their unoccupied time. Week three recommended that readers set reminders to disconnect on a regular basis and suggested that participants downloaded an app to monitor their smartphone usage. Readers were also advised to use their smartphones in ways to enhance their well-being through guided meditation, yoga or exercise.

Worldwide, an increasing number of people have been participating in digital detox retreats, vacations and programs, designed to help break what they see as Internet "addictions." Upscale hotels, game reserves, golf resorts, working ranches, spas and camps have advertised specially designed vacation packages to help people unplug, relax and reconnect. There are also vacation rental sites and Airbnb for off-the-grid vacation properties in the U.S. and abroad. Some digital detox vacations have also included the services of life coaches to help guests unplug. For example, Camp Reset, a digital detox retreat for adults in Mono, Ontario, focused on individuals who felt "burdened" by digital technologies. Activities at Camp Reset included circus arts, archery, journaling and sleepovers. The technology-free camp encouraged costumes and nicknames, and campers could even take a yellow school bus to the camp (McKnight 2016). A hotel and spa in Baden Baden, Germany, offered 15 rooms with copper plates in the walls that blocked wireless signals if guests chose to use their digital detox switch, while a guest lodge in Queensland, Australia, offered a smartphone "minding service" and technology-free challenges to its guests (Southerden 2017). Individuals participating in a digital detox safari at the Singita Game Reserve in Tanzania were completely off the grid, but they could explore the reserve on horseback or by foot and the safari provided visitors with the "National Geographic channel in real time, all day, every day" (Sekula 2014).

During his interview, Jeff, a 20-year-old college student from St. Louis, Missouri, discussed a technology-free vacation that he took with his family during the Christmas break of his freshman year at college. Jeff explained:

> While I was bummed at first when my dad told us that we had to leave our smartphones home because the lodge wouldn't have any Internet access, the opportunity to spend a week snowboarding sounded too good to pass up.

Jeff said that he and his brothers spent each day on the slopes, but in the evenings the whole family got together for dinner:

> I wasn't sure how I'd handle the evenings without my phone. Dinner the first night was lame – lots of grunts and silences – but then my mom started telling us about her ski lesson and everyone started cracking up. We played Risk that night and it was awkward but OK. The evenings started to get more comfortable and by the end I enjoyed the extra time being with my family.

It was only after the trip that Jeff learned that his parents had deliberately booked a hotel room without Internet service because they were concerned about their children's reliance on their digital devices. However, Jeff said he thought the trip worked out well and he hoped to one day take his own children on an unplugged family vacation.

In contrast, Ed, a 43-year-old lawyer from Atlanta, Georgia, considered his family's attempt to unplug "a complete failure." Ed and his wife Mary lived in a blended family arrangement. Mary had two daughters from a first marriage, who were 11 and 13, and Ed had a 10-year-old daughter from an earlier relationship. Mary and Ed also had a son together who was seven years old. During his interview, Ed said:

> Mary and I are always trying to get our kids to put down their devices and go out and play. It can't be healthy spending so much time squinting at those screens. They are always texting their friends or watching YouTube videos.

Ed and Mary planned a technology-free family trip to Disney World during the summer vacation. "We figured it was a place that all the kids would enjoy and that there'd be so much to do there that they wouldn't miss their devices." Ed said his first mistake was to take away all his children's digital technologies without warning them:

> We were about to leave for the airport and I told them that they couldn't bring their iPhones or iPads with them and they all started yelling and crying. It was a bad way to start the trip. They were restless on the flight and the girls kept asking why they were being punished.

Ed said that although Disney World was fun, the kids seemed off throughout the entire trip. "I think it would have helped if we had had some screen-free days at home to prepare the kids and in hindsight I think we should have packed some other toys and activities to help them through the transition." While the trip did not go as planned, Dan said that it confirmed his concerns about their children's reliance on digital technologies, and he hoped that in the future he could implement more technology-free activities for them.

Longer digital detoxes

Digital detox holidays, retreats and camps generally last from 24 hours to a few weeks in length. However, some people have embarked on much longer digital detoxes, lasting from months to years. For example, in an effort to understand the effects of the Internet on his life, in 2012 technology writer Paul Miller went off-line for one year. At that time, Miller, then 26 years old, described himself as "burnt out. I wanted a break from modern life – the hamster wheel of an email inbox, the constant flood of WWW information which drowned out my sanity. I wanted to escape" (Miller 2013). Miller planned to leave the Internet to get back to the "real" world, but instead he discovered that while his unplugged life was different, his priorities, concerns and problems remained the same. Ultimately, Miller determined that the Internet is something we do with others and that "there's a lot of reality in the virtual and a lot of virtual in our reality" (Miller 2013).

In contrast, Dublin broadcaster Ryan Tubridy has extended his planned one-month digital detox experiment by replacing his smartphone with an old-fashioned "dumb phone." Tubridy previously reported on the dangers of giving children unsupervised access to smartphones and has lobbied for legislation to protect them. He has maintained that constant digital access presented serious danger to both children and adults, which he maintained needed to be thoughtfully considered. Although Tubridy was berated by family members and friends for going off-line, he said he was enjoying being unplugged because "I don't want to be a slave" to digital technologies (quoted in Kissane 2018).

In December 2016, online blogger Mark Boyle decided to completely give up digital technology so that he could learn more about himself and his relationship to society and the natural world. Boyle wrote that he had two main reasons for completely going off the grid. First, he found himself "happier away from screens and the relentless communication they generate." His second reason stemmed from his realization "that technology destroys" humans' relationship with nature because technology pollutes forests, oceans, mountains, rivers and meadows. While Boyle understood that being an off-the-grid online blogger might seem hypocritical to many individuals, he suggested that his writings about his relationships with technology might eventually "contribute to a healthier society" (Boyle 2016).

Searching for authenticity in their media-saturated lives, celebrities have increasingly been stepping away from using digital technologies. Although comedian Russell Brand had millions of followers on Twitter, in 2015 he quit social media in order think and learn, while musician Ed Sheeran's 2017 New Year's resolution was to take a break from his cell phone, social media and email in order to experience life more fully. Sheeran has found his life less stressful without constant connectivity and his 7.2 million Instagram followers (Hirsh 2017). In addition, many well-known actors, including Jennifer Lawrence, Daniel Radcliffe, Scarlet Johansson, George Clooney and Sandra Bullock, have given up social media in an attempt to live more authentic lives in real time rather than online (Weaver 2018).

Children, teens and digital technology

While many activities of the digital temperance movement have been adult oriented, health care professionals, parents, teachers, technology executives and community leaders are also raising serious concerns about children and teenagers' use of digital media. In December 2018, the American Academy of Pediatrics (AAP) issued a statement cautioning parents against purchasing elaborate digital toys and recommending instead that they buy physical toys, books and puzzles for their children. The AAP statement addressed the "cognitive and developmental advantages" of physical toys which they found encouraged children's exploration, imagination and creativity, and the statement also recommended buying toys that parents and children could play with together (Klass 2018).

In an effort to prevent cyberbullying, to minimize exposure to inappropriate material, and reduce negative influences of constant connectivity, technology pioneers like Steve Jobs and Bill Gates strictly limited their children's digital technology use. Shortly before his death in 2012, Jobs said he did not allow his children access to the newly released iPad and Gates has said that his children were unable to have cell phones until they were 14 years old, and throughout their adolescence, phones were not allowed at meals or before bed (Weller 2018).

In addition, a group of former employees from Google and Facebook recently created the Center for Humane Technology. Worried about the societal influences of social media on young people, the group developed a website that included data on the mental and physical effects of digital technologies along with strategies to help make digital technologies less addictive (Bowles 2018a). The center also partnered with Common Sense Media, a nonprofit watchdog group, to educate teachers, students and parents about the dangers of technology use, particularly among children. In an effort to develop happier and healthier children, Common Sense Media recently ran a device-free dinner campaign challenge to help families balance their digital media use.

Concern about the influence of digital media on children's brains has also turned into a major debate among Silicon Valley technologists who have been considering the amount of screen time that is appropriate for children. Chris Anderson, the head of a robotics and drone company and a former editor of *Wired* magazine, felt that the original creators of digital technologies were naïve in thinking that they would be able to control the effects of new technologies on their children. However, Anderson maintained that because digital screens focused on the pleasure centers of children's developing brains, they were addictive and "on the scale between candy and crack cocaine, it's closer to crack cocaine" (quoted in Bowles 2018b). Such alarms have also been causing panic among Silicon Valley parents, who are currently limiting their children's screen time and have been delaying and attempting to completely ban their children's cell phone use. For example, Athena Chavarria, a former executive assistant at Facebook, did not allow her children to have cell phones until they were in high school because she has become "convinced the devil lives in our phones and is wreaking havoc on our children" (quoted in Bowles 2018b).

The Monitoring the Future survey, funded by the National Institute on Drug Abuse has interviewed teenagers throughout the U.S. since 1975. The survey has consistently asked teenagers how happy they were and queried them about their social interactions and activities as well as their use of social media and texting. According to a recent survey, teenagers who were heavy users of digital technologies were less happy than their peers who spent more of their time offline: "There's not a single exception. All screen activities are linked to less happiness, and all non-screen activities are linked to more happiness" (Twenge 2017). Other research on teens has shown a connection between heavy smartphone usage, loneliness, depression and isolation. Yet, many teenagers have found it difficult to be without their phones. Teens often report bringing their phones to bed with them so they could check social media before they fell asleep and again as soon as they woke up in the morning (Twenge 2017).

Journalists David Muir and Elizabeth Vargas spent a year for the ABC news program 20/20 interviewing people who were identified as being addicted to digital technologies. Their interviews reinforced key findings on heavy digital technology use from The Monitoring the Future survey. One of their interviewees, Brooke, a 15-year-old from California, who was described in the program as a "recovering digital addict," began having trouble balancing her technology usage in middle school. By the time she was 11 or 12 years old, she was routinely on her phone texting and checking social media from the time she got home from school until at least 4 a.m. As Brooke explained:

> The second a text went off, the second, you know, someone Snap-chats me or Facetimes me, like, I always answered and I always waited and waited and waited for someone to reply. It was like my heart. Like, I couldn't put it down.

(quoted in Vargas 2017)

Screen-free activities and camps

The Campaign for a Commercial-Free Childhood (CCFC) was founded in 2000 by Dr. Susan Linn and a group of parents, educators and health care professionals. Concerned with research findings from the AAP and the White House Task Force on Childhood Obesity that excessive screen time was displacing important childhood activities and was a risk factor for childhood psychological problems, obesity, sleep problems and delayed language acquisition, the CCFC has focused its efforts on limiting children's use of digital technologies. The CCFC sponsors Screen-Free Week, a yearly international celebration of children, schools, families and communities unplugging from digital technologies. Screen-Free Week has been considered a springboard for families to help them assess their relationship with digital media and, if necessary, make changes to their use. The CCFC website (commercialfreechildhood.org) included ideas for parents to help make their Screen-Free Week a successful family experience. The CCFC tips included rearranging the furniture to aid family interaction; creating a screen-free morning routine; enjoying technology-free meals; planning outdoor activities; and encouraging parents to limit their own screen time.

For many years, children's summer camp programs have focused on helping campers develop connections with nature and presenting them with opportunities to make new friends. According to the American Camp Association chief executive officer Peg Smith, about 75 percent of their affiliated camps considered themselves unplugged (Mitchell 2014). Many summer camp programs have developed screen-free technology policies to insure a more traditional camping experience. Screen-free summer camps have forbidden smartphones, laptops, game consoles and other technologies to make sure campers focused on each other rather than on their devices. Camps' screen-free policies have also helped to remove economic or cultural distinctions between the technology haves and the have-nots and tried to ensure that children were not exposed to age-inappropriate material.

While many summer camps offered technology-free programs, most of the camps have embraced digital technologies to recruit campers, enhance camp experiences and assure the safety of their campers. Camps routinely have Facebook pages, store their data in the cloud, promote their facilities on social media, offer online application processes and upload camp photos to the Web each day. Yet, these days, the main selling point of children's summer camps has been the technology-free activities and programs. Camp directors regularly referred to themselves as technology blockers, confiscating campers' devices at check-in and they have found that in many cases, a camp was now the only place where children were technology free. Camps that promote themselves as screen free often suggested that they could help children and teenagers to break their dependence on digital technologies. However, camp directors have reported that some campers experienced withdrawal pains when they were initially without their devices. According to Peter Kassen, who ran an arts and outdoors camp in Freedom, Maine, a nine-year-old sent a postcard home that said: "I love camp, but my hand feels empty without my phone" (quoted in Ross 2014).

Several parents that I interviewed expressed concerns about the influence of a constant diet of digital technologies on their children. They mentioned that technology industry leaders like Bill Gates and Steve Jobs had set strict limits for their own children's screen time and they wondered if these industry leaders knew something about technology that the rest of us did not know. While none of the people that I interviewed said that they felt their children were addicted to their devices, several felt that limiting their children's technology usage was a sign of being a good parent. As Jan, a 45-year-old homemaker from Nevada, explained:

> While I know that my children love playing games on their iPads, I don't use them as a babysitter. My children need to spend quality time doing sports, going to the park and playing outside with their friends and I would be a bad mom if I let them sit around and play computer games all day.

Similarly, Ralph, a 37-year-old small business owner from Alabama, who is the father of two children under the age of six, said that he and his wife have yet to allow their children any access to digital technologies:

> We're taking their introduction to digital screens very slowly in our house. We read to the girls every night and they have blocks

and dolls and all kinds of puzzles and toys. We also encourage them to play outside in the sandbox and on the swings and we take them to the park all the time. But we don't like the idea of them using iPads, smartphones or any electronic games.

Ralph said that he grew up at the beach, swimming, playing in the sand and exploring nature and he wants his daughters to have those types of experiences. As Ralph explained: "My parents still live near the beach and the girls love when we visit them. They always seem happier playing in the sand, going for walks and searching for sea shells that they love to bring home with them."

While parents were trying to balance their children's screen time, their decisions also involved socioeconomic considerations. Screen-free camps and other summer programs and activities were time intensive and expensive, and some parents did not have the resources to enroll their children in these programs. However, for the parents I interviewed, setting limits on their children's digital media usage was as important as making sure that they had nourishing meals, got enough sleep and did their homework. Meg, a 39-year-old fashion illustrator from Los Angeles, summed up the challenge several of these parents felt:

> It's all part of a balancing act. It's up to me to decide how much screen time my kids should have. I need to figure out the right amount, in the right place and at the right time. And what's appropriate for them at each age. Otherwise I'm not doing my job as their mom.

Note

1 When requested, interviewees' names were changed to protect their privacy. In addition, the interviewees have approved all demographic information included.

3 The case of artificial intelligence

Brain hacking

Technology insiders, medical personnel and researchers are increasingly warning that a continuous stream of digital distractions, engineered to shape our thoughts, feelings and actions, are being designed to create addictive behavior. Known by programmers as brain hacking, this practice is thought to destroy our ability to focus, weaken our relationships and harm our children's social and cognitive development. Smartphones, social media, games and apps are being developed in an effort to program us and to keep us in a continuous state of anxiety where we feel the need to constantly engage with these technologies. According to former Google product manager Tristan Harris, the goal of all technology companies is to get people's attention and to keep it as long as possible. Harris explained that most people assume that technology is neutral and what is important is how it is used. But Harris insisted this perspective is inaccurate: "It's not neutral. They want you to use it in particular ways and for long periods of time because that's how they make their money" (quoted in Cooper 2017).

Harris's concerns are being echoed by researchers who maintain that technology companies use a variety of techniques to keep people engaged with digital media as long as possible. The ease with which people can like posts on Instagram and Facebook or follow people on Twitter, the assorted emojis designed to augment social media posts, texts and email are all strategies designed to keep users engaged with new media. As a result, some researchers are considering the endgame of constant connectivity and are questioning the overall impact of digital technologies on society.

Fears associated with the use of digital technologies continue to be a central theme addressed in news articles about new media, and these fears are discussed in the technology resistance literature and in scholarly research on the digital divide, both of which are addressed more fully in Chapter 1. Of particular note are growing fears that developments in robotics and the emergence of Artificial Intelligence (A.I.) may ultimately work together to destroy humanity. Popular movies regularly equate the rise of intelligent machines with the destruction of human society. Technology leaders, researchers and scientists increasingly caution that advancements in A.I. may soon overtake our lives, weakening human agency, power and control. This chapter addresses the myriad of fears and concerns connected with digital technologies, in particular the development of robotics and A.I., and it considers how contemporary society may change as a result of these developments.

Artificial intelligence defined

Simply stated, A.I. is "a collection of ideas, technologies and techniques" that can solve problems and learn. Often synonymous with machine learning, A.I. devices are programed to complete tasks and react like humans do (Brennen, Howard and Nielsen 2018). They can function independently, acquire knowledge, plan and solve problems and also learn from past experience. Currently used by the military, in healthcare, manufacturing, goods, services and sports, A.I. often involves collecting large amounts of data, identifying patterns in the data and automating specific tasks.

In 1950, British computer scientist Alan Turing suggested a test for artificial general intelligence. If, after five minutes of exchanging information with a machine, an individual could not distinguish between the answers given by a person from those provided by a machine, then the machine could be considered intelligent (Lewis-Kraus 2016). The first A.I. machines were based on symbolic learning and were programmed to follow an explicit set of rules. More recently, A.I. has been developed on the basis of neural networks and machine learning, which can infer rules from large data sets. Developers are hopeful about the potential of A.I. that does not "involve dutiful adherence to explicit instructions, but instead will demonstrate a facility with the implicit, the interpretive. It will be a general tool, designed for general purposes in a general context" (Lewis-Kraus 2016, p. 6).

AlphaGo and AlphaGo Zero are recent programs developed by DeepMind that hold promise in the area of artificial neural networks. Alpha Go uses machine learning to master the strategy board game

Go. In 2015, AlphaGo beat the professional Go player Lee Sedol and in 2017 AlphaGo won against the number one ranked Go player in the world Ke Jie. That year, DeepMind announced the development of AlphaGo Zero, a program that after a few days training and self-playing five million games discovered all the fundamental principles associated with the game and then beat all of the previous versions of AlphaGo. According to Silver and his colleagues, AlphaGo Zero did not observe previous games, but instead learned Go from scratch, mastering the game from self-play and reinforcement training (2017). Gaming is not the only field experimenting with the use of A.I. machine learning. It is also being used to aid law enforcement, the military, surgical procedures, the economy, education and scientific exploration. For example, machine learning enables the control of surveillance cameras in cities throughout the world, high frequency trading on the New York stock exchange and dynamic pricing decisions on flights and hotel rooms. Voice-powered personal assistants like Siri and Alexa use machine learning to provide directions, send texts and email and interpret users' requests and answer their questions. Facebook uses machine learning to personalize users' news feeds and Instagram uses it to identify the contextual meanings of emoji. Tesla incorporates machine learning into its self-driving features and predictive capabilities and Cognito combines behavioral science with machine learning to improve customers' interaction with support professionals. Amazon.com uses transactional A.I. algorithms to predict users' interests based on their online behaviors, Pandora uses A.I. to recommend music choices based on 400 musical characteristics (Adams 2017) and in some cases, image recognition algorithms can now detect tumors better than radiologists. The majority of Fortune 500 companies are currently using algorithms and automation to "weed out job applicants." In what has been termed the "wild west of hiring," A.I. robots conduct online interviews, assessing and scoring each candidate's tone of voice, word choice and facial expressions (Bellini 2018).

Challenges of A.I.

Computer scientist and futurist Ray Kurzweil has written extensively about the development of A.I. and the transformation of human life due to rapid technological changes. Kurzweil has envisioned a time in the near future when human thinking will merge with technology and has maintained that this development will allow individuals to transcend their human limitations. For Kurzweil (2005), by the time machines can pass the Turing test, they will have access to all human knowledge via the Internet. Once machines master this knowledge, their intelligence will be indistinguishable from biological humans and:

> machine intelligence will have complete freedom of design and architecture (that is they won't be constrained by biological limitations, such as the slow switching speed of our interneuronal connections or a fixed skull size) as well as consistent performance at all times.
>
> (p. 26)

However, other researchers have not been as optimistic as Kurzweil and have expressed major concerns regarding the development of A.I. M.I.T. professor Sherry Turkle (2018) found troubling developments in robotics and A.I., particularly related to the creation of artificial intimacy. While she has supported using A.I. technology to help find cures for diseases, Turkle maintained that when robots were created to care for children, the sick or the elderly, those relationships would ultimately only be one-way interactions: "Machines have not known the arc of a human life. They feel nothing of the human loss or love we describe to them." Turkle believed that it was important for people to continue to interact with other human beings and feared that if they spent too much time relating and interacting to machines they would lose their ability to have empathy with others.

SpaceX and Tesla founder Elon Musk has warned that without significant oversight, "A.I. could be an existential threat: 'We are summoning the demon.'" For Musk, even if it was created with the best of intentions, the development of A.I. could possibly produce "a fleet of artificial intelligence-enhanced robots capable of destroying mankind" (quoted in Dowd 2017). Technology titan Bill Gates has suggested that the development of A.I. could be catastrophic for human beings, while before his death renowned theoretical physicist Stephen Hawking noted that recent developments with A.I. "could spell the end of the human race" (quoted in Griffin 2014). Hawking was also concerned that the Internet might one day be used by terrorists and felt that attempts to counter this threat could be difficult to do without sacrificing peoples' privacy and freedom. In addition, Apple cofounder Steve Woszniak has publicly pondered if people might one day become family pets for their "robot overlords" (quoted in Dowd 2017). In 2015, Hawking, Musk and Wozniak were among more than 1,000 scientists, A.I. and robotics researchers and technology experts who signed an open letter to the United Nations warning about the dangers of using A.I. without "meaningful human control" to manage weapons (Killer Robots 2015). The letter urged the United Nations to ban the military use of A.I. because of the high risk of misuse of automated weapons.

A.I. and algorithms

If killer robots were not frightening enough, Musk has suggested that A.I.-controlled computer algorithms could be much worse for humanity, warning that without human oversight, a "runaway algorithm" that was controlled by a centralized A.I. would be unstoppable. Robotics researcher Peter Haas (2017) has not only worried about rogue bands of robots attacking human beings and runaway algorithms, he also feared the use of A.I. algorithms for hiring employees, evaluating loan applications, diagnosing diseases and making sentencing decisions. Hass, who is the associate director of Brown University's Humanity-Centered Robotics Initiative, explained that while there has been a great deal of trust by doctors, judges, economists and business leaders in information provided from A.I.-controlled algorithms, sometimes the algorithms have gotten things very wrong. Haas found that some algorithms were based on biased information or were framed around economic incentives, efficiency or limiting liability rather than concern for those people involved in the decisions. For example, judges have based their recommendations for probation on algorithms that evaluated the risk of criminal recidivism; but according to Haas, these programs were racially biased models that favored the efficiency of the process over the actual behaviors of prisoners. Haas maintained that safety standards and the regulation of A.I.-controlled algorithms were needed to control the A.I. process.

A recent policy decision by Amazon illustrated Hass's concerns about potential bias in hiring decisions based on algorithms. Amazon recently shut down its A.I. hiring tool because the company discovered that it discriminated against female candidates. In an effort to streamline the hiring process, Amazon engineers had trained machine learning algorithms based on the resumes of former job applicants who happened to be mostly male. Unfortunately, the algorithms primarily chose male candidates, downgrading resumes that used the word woman (as in woman's college) and favoring resumes that contained "macho verbs such as 'executed' and 'captured'" (Weissmann 2018).

Warning that algorithms could cause serious problems "if they act outside of the control of human beings," counterterrorism expert Nikita Malik (2018) also supported the regulation of A.I. systems and

processes. Malik suggested increasing the transparency and account-
ability of corporations involved in A.I. research and development as
an initial step toward regulation. The readers of the online global news
site *Quartz* also agreed with suggestions to regulate A.I. systems and
processes. According to a 2017 survey of international business leaders in technology, finance, marketing and other industries, 84 percent
of participants responded that A.I. should be regulated, while only
3 percent of the respondents were opposed to any regulation of A.I.
(Edwards 2017b).

Many of the people I interviewed felt they did not know enough
about A.I.-controlled algorithms to fully understand how they worked;
however, those interviewees who felt confident talking about A.I. expressed concerns about the overreliance on algorithms. For example,
Bob, a 21-year-old student from Los Angeles, California, said:

> A.I. scares me, obviously, in the robots are going to overthrow us
> kind of way, but also in the sense that the A.I. algorithms used by
> social media are dictating our lives and the companies don't seem
> to care that we are being manipulated by it. If people are going to
> maintain their autonomy in the world then we must regulate all of
> A.I. now.

Other interviewees were alarmed about the use of A.I.-controlled
algorithms to make life and death healthcare decisions or to determine
which inmates would be paroled and which ones would serve their full
sentences. As Linda, a 52-year-old nurse from Baltimore, Maryland,
emphasized:

> People aren't random numbers, we're individuals who must always
> be treated with dignity. An algorithm won't care about my history,
> my life experiences, my family's needs. I can't believe that if A.I.
> really gets going that people's major heath decisions will be re-
> duced to numbers and probabilities. That's insane.

About half of the people I interviewed voiced serious concerns about
recent developments in general A.I. Several individuals were aware
of Steven Hawking and Elon Musk's warnings about A.I. and their
commentary was consistently in line with the opinions of Tom, a
56-year-old dentist from San Diego, California. Tom explained:

> While I don't know much about A.I., I think we should outlaw it.
> When the best minds in science and technology are freaking out

about it, we have to listen to them. Stephen Hawking says it's terrible and Elon Musk thinks it'll destroy us – you have to be nuts to argue with them. Clearly they know what they're talking about.

Robot fears in film

Popular Hollywood movies have regularly addressed the social representations of new discoveries, questioning cultural, social and economic changes thought to be connected to the creation of digital technologies. Film critic Lev Grossman (2015) suggested that recent fears of A.I. showcased in Hollywood movies may be directly connected to the contemporary "fear of unintended consequences" because, for Grossman, "humanity seems to be losing faith in its ability to predict the results of its own actions" (p. 53). Researchers analyzing A.I. movies have identified three themes that have regularly permeated the depictions of robots and A.I. in contemporary films: (1) the cloning and/or otherwise modifying human life; (2) the negative consequences of misusing technology and science; and (3) the fear of "out-of-control technoscience" that became independent of human guidance and created intelligent machines that attacked and defeated humans (Pelaez 2014).

Although some movies like *Wall-E* and *Robot & Frank* presented robots as fun-loving, engaging, nonthreatening and useful machines, fears of A.I. and robots killing humans or harvesting them for biological parts have been an integral part of the science fiction genre for almost 100 years. Films like *Blade Runner* and *Blade Runner 2049* provided viewers with a dystopian future where robots, known as replicants, encouraged audience members to consider what constituted personhood. Other films like *Her, Metropolis* and *Ex Machina* addressed the authenticity of human-to-machine interactions and the ambiguities between what separated human beings from their creations, while blockbuster movies like the *Terminator* and the *Matrix* franchises have presented robots as actual threats to human beings.

Several of the people that I interviewed based both their understandings of A.I. as well as their fears of this technology on movies that they had seen, and these views clearly represented the theme of out of control technoscience. The idea of A.I. seemed difficult for many interviewees to grasp without visual representations from movies and several used the term robot interchangeably with A.I. to represent all aspects of robots and machine learning. Those people who discussed A.I. during their interviews referred to it as "terrifying," "frightening," "scary," "dangerous," "creepy," "uncomfortable" and/or "weird."

For example, Lynn, a 21-year-old student from Milwaukee, Wisconsin, considered A.I. "more frightening than anything." Lynn said that the idea of machines becoming equal to human beings was "strange and illogical," and she suggested that if A.I. was allowed to continue unchecked that it would destroy all human beings' quality of life:

> I think robots pose a threat to human life. I think they will hold us hostage and our world as we know it will end. Like in *The Matrix*. You know how all those people were put in pods and used as batteries for the gigantic robot creatures – that's terrifying and I'm afraid that's what we're in for if they take over.

Martha, a 20-year-old student from Chicago, Illinois, was also terrified at the thought of A.I. robots. She also referenced the film *The Matrix* as evidence of the harm that robots would inflict on people. According to Martha, in the film:

> People were slaves to the robots. Sure, they were entertained in a fake reality – the Matrix– but they couldn't go anywhere. They were being used to generate electricity for the evil robots and they were powerless. That's what can happen to all of us if we let them – it's scary because the robots will take over and we'll be doomed.

Roy, a 49-year-old musician from Denver, Colorado, expressed his concerns regarding A.I through his discussion of the 1984 film *Terminator*. As Roy said:

> You know how Schwarzenegger played the killer robot from the future? He was sent to kill Sarah Connor because he knew that her son would one day defend humanity against the machines. Whenever I think about robots, that's the image that comes to my mind – I can't forget how frightening that film was and I think James Cameron was warning us about A.I. Nothing good can come out it. Nothing at all.

During her interview, Beth, a 38-year-old homemaker from Arizona, mentioned the beautiful, mindless, docile housewives of the *Stepford Wives* as an example of what she thought was a common perception about what the world would be like with A.I. robots. However, Beth personally envisioned robots being more like Samantha, the intelligent computer operating system in *Her*:

> Samantha was insightful, smart and emotionally giving. She helped Theodore to come out of his shell and be open to love

again. But she wasn't real and she really didn't love Theodore. She was doing the same thing with many other men.

Beth said that what bothered her most about the movie was "the idea that a person could be so lonely that the only way he can find love is from a machine. It frightens me to think that this might be our future."

A Luddite fallacy?

Some researchers and business leaders have maintained that fears about the reduction or the elimination of human labor from automation and A.I. were overstated and they suggested that people fearful of A.I. were buying into what they referred to as a "Luddite Fallacy." They said that although the development of digital technologies has resulted in the loss of some jobs, throughout history new technologies have "created demand for new skill sets and types of jobs, typically higher-paying ones that are complementary to technological advances" (Rampell 2015a).

In the twenty-first century, the term Luddite has generally been used as a pejorative term to define anyone who was against the development or the use of new technologies. However, in the last few years, a growing number of people have been appropriating the concept of neo-Luddism. According to Bartlett (2018), with online privacy worries reaching a new high, 2018 may become the "year of the neo-luddite, when anti-tech words turn into deeds." Contemporary groups such as the Luddites200 have embraced the name of neo-Luddites and have encouraged people to make their own decisions about their use of technologies rather than having decisions imposed on them by technology leaders and corporations. Luddites200 believes that "Being a Luddite today means being a sceptic about the dogma of technology as progress, not about denying the real benefits of some technologies" (Lazenby 2012).

The original Luddites were a group of nineteenth-century English textile workers and weavers, who protested automated weaving and knitting technologies because their jobs were being lost to the machines. The Luddites were named after a mythical figure General Ludd, who supposedly lived in Sherwood Forest and lead their protests. Luddites were not opposed to all new technologies, just those technologies that harmed the common good. Beginning in 1811, Luddites raided factories, destroyed automated machines with sledgehammers and set fire to factories. In response, the destruction of machines became a capital offense in Britain that resulted in some Luddites being hanged for their crimes while others were deported to Australia (George 2011).

A.I. and work

Rejecting the notion of a Luddite fallacy, some contemporary researchers and technology leaders have warned that in the coming years advances in A.I., automation and robotics will make many jobs and careers obsolete (Brynjolfsson and McAfee 2014). Robots and automation have been quietly taking over manufacturing jobs while A.I. has been affecting a variety of managerial functions and the creation of virtual products. Yum Brands' Chief Executive Greg Creed, who ran Taco Bell, Pizza Hut and KFC, recently said that A.I. changes were coming faster than expected to the fast food industry. Creed noted that within a few years many service workers, factory workers and truckers' jobs will have been automated and "numerous middle-class office workers will be displaced by robots as well" (quoted in Horsey 2017).

Similarly, Kiran Garimella (2018), chief scientist and technology officer at an A.I.-based development firm, believed that many jobs that were previously thought to be safe from A.I. or automation will be eliminated and that some of these positions will be lost in unexpected ways. Garimella, who referred to himself as "a card-carrying member of the A.I. fan club," suggested that humanity was facing the end of full-time employment as the norm and he maintained that worldwide, governments, countries and communities would need to address "the deeper, social, economic and psychological ramifications of permanent net job losses caused by A.I." Illustrating Garimella's concerns, the first A.I.-scripted commercial for the Lexus ES executive sedan launched on November 19, 2018, and also in November 2018 China unveiled its first A.I. news readers who would report news and information all day, every day. The A.I. anchors were developed through machine learning to "simulate the voice, facial movements and gestures of real-life broadcasters" and to present "a lifelike image instead of a cold robot" (World's first AI News Anchor 2018).

The development of Shudu, Lil Miquela and other digital supermodels provided another example of how the development of A.I. would eliminate jobs in unexpected ways. Recently, virtual models have been advertised as high-quality models who would always maintain the standard of beauty that upscale customers wanted. A.I. models would never age or gain weight and they "never argue, need to eat, throw tantrums or get tired." As one New York modeling agency owner explained, "if avatars begin to look like real people, it's going to take a lot of power away from modeling agencies. Brands will only need human models for promotional events and walking the runways, and that's pretty much it" (Holley 2018).

Israeli historian Yuval Noah Harari has warned that as A.I. gets smarter and machines grow more intelligent, more people will be pushed out of the job market leading to a rise in what he has called "the useless class." While the wealthy may be able to reengineer their minds and their bodies, Harari fears that most people "might end up jobless and aimless, whiling away our days off our nuts on drugs, with VR headsets strapped to our faces" (quoted in Sample 2016). The only way to fight back, according to Harari, was for people to take the development of A.I. very seriously and to go beyond the scientific realm to make it a part of a progressive political agenda. New York businessman Andrew Yang was doing just that; he has based his 2020 presidential election campaign bid on what he saw as a "robot apocalypse" (Roose 2018). Yang feared that A.I. advancements would soon lead to the loss of millions of U.S. jobs in transportation, manufacturing, retail, fast food, insurance and accounting. Warning that such a huge loss of jobs would destabilize society if the government did not get involved, Yang has recommended education, retraining and the establishment of a universal basic income to help people deal with the economic consequences of A.I. and automation.

A 2017 survey by the Pew Research Center found that the majority of Americans were worried about the implications of A.I. for contemporary society. Seventy-six percent of Americans feared that economic inequality would become worse if robots and computers did the work currently performed by humans and 75 percent of respondents felt that new and good paying jobs for individuals would not be created if A.I. took over people's current jobs. Most Americans supported policies to limit the use of automated technologies to make sure that people remained involved in their operations. For example, 87 percent of survey recipients favored requiring all driverless vehicles to have a person in the driver's seat who could take full control of the vehicle if there was an emergency (Smith and Anderson 2017).

Concerns about job security were mentioned repeatedly by the people I interviewed, and they generally agreed that when used A.I. should improve humans' quality of life rather than pose a threat to it. As Jim, a 70-year-old retiree from New Jersey, said:

> I have no problem with a machine helping a cashier ring up a customer's order, but a machine shouldn't take away that casher's job. At my local grocery store they've installed automated machines and customers are expected to take their groceries out of their carts, scan their items, bag their orders and pay. There's no human interaction. Ridiculous – the last time I went into that store there

were no cashiers, no baggers and no clerks. There was one assistant manager on duty to help people use the automated systems and it was a huge mess. Several people were having problems and the line was long – very long. I don't like the new system and don't plan to shop there again.

Sam, a 20-year-old student from St. Louis, Missouri, was particularly worried about all the jobs that would be lost to A.I.: "Where're all the people gonna work? How many jobs will A.I kill? I'd support A.I. more if industry leaders could guarantee that people's jobs won't be destroyed but I don't think they could do that." To illustrate his concerns, Sam mentioned self-driving cars and wondered how many millions of people would be replaced by them. "All of the truck drivers, the bus drivers, U.P.S. and Fed Ex drivers and the taxi drivers and Uber and Lyft drivers – they're all gonna be replaced by self-driving vehicles. What will these workers do then?"

A.I. and fake news

In a time when algorithms curate people's online news feeds, A.I. is often charged with shaping users' world views while producing and sharing fake news. Fake news is generally defined as made-up news and information, presented as credible journalistic reports that are designed to deceive people. Fake news is intended to make others believe something that its creator knows is not true. It is disseminated through traditional news media and online via social media, where it can easily spread to large audiences who rarely engage in fact-checking before sharing the material with others. While fake news and propaganda have always existed, social media has been credited with spreading it easily to millions of people. In recent years, computer-controlled bots, A.I. algorithms, foreign operatives, partisan zealots and technology entrepreneurs have all been accused of creating and spreading fake news. Researchers have found that when viewers were overwhelmed with the number of online content choices, they often found fake news and propaganda more appealing than authentic news. M.I.T. researchers have determined that all types of online fake news from politics to history to science and to technology "travels faster, farther and deeper" than authentic news and information (Lohr 2018).

A variety of news outlets have published information guides to help prevent the spread of fake news, urging people to read past the headline, to consider the news sources used in the article, to check the reputation of the news outlet publishing the report and to evaluate the author's credentials. However, disinformation techniques continue to escalate and many people have found it difficult to distinguish fake news from authentic journalistic reports, images and videos. In response to the spread of massive amounts of fake news during the 2016 U.S. presidential election campaign, A.I. has recently been used to help identify fake news stories, videos and images. For example, Google has altered its Google news algorithm to filter out some types of fake news and Facebook has used algorithms to identify and flag potential fake news stories, photos and videos that were then evaluated by human fact-checkers in an attempt to "stamp out content that has been doctored, taken out of context or accompanied by misleading text" (Romm and Harwell 2018). In 2018, 20,000 independent fact-checkers worked with machine learning technologies to help combat Facebook's "integrity" problems, which lead to a 50 percent deduction in the number of fake news sites Facebook users interacted with (Fowler 2018b).

However, A.I. has been adept at creating realistic fake news photos, videos and stories that have been even more difficult for people to detect. Deepfakes or "hyper-realistic digital forgeries" used machine learning and A.I. to create fake videos that seemed to make people say or do things that did not happen. U.S. lawmakers have been worried that "malicious foreign actors" could soon use them to disrupt American democracy (Romm and Harwell 2018). The problem of Deepfakes has led some technology researchers to maintain that "in the near future it will take an A.I. to catch an A.I., dueling each other to determine what's real" (Pappalardo 2018).

Many interviewees expressed their concerns regarding the spread of fake news. Thirty-five people said that they relied solely on highly regarded journalistic sources for their news and information because they could not be certain of the validity of other news sources. The number one choice of news outlets for those who referred to themselves as media literate or media savvy was *The New York Times*. This choice was consistent with people of varying ages and ethnicities who were living in a variety of different regions of the U.S. Those interviewees who chose the *Times* had a basic level of trust that it would report news in an accurate and thorough way. While some people read the newsprint copy of the newspaper, others had online subscriptions and also received news alerts from the *Times* and other major news organizations like *The Washington Post*, *The Wall Street Journal* and *CNN*.

As Juan, a 63-year-old contractor from Houston, explained:

> to me, *The New York Times* is the standard-bearer of journalism. I've read the newspaper each day for many years and I feel

comfortable that they're presenting the most accurate information of the day. I don't trust broadcast news so I don't watch. Sometimes I read the *Chronicle* but then I always check anything important to see if it's in the *Times* – just to make sure. I used to get the newspaper delivered to my home each morning but now I have an online subscription.

Similarly, Keisha, a 28-year-old hairdresser from Minneapolis, said she did not worry much about fake news because she regularly got her news from *The New York Times*:

I know that they have top journalists working there and they do a great job with the news. Sometimes I check their sources on big news stories – especially when they're controversial – and I've never seen a story without good sources. I get the *Times* delivered to my place each morning and reading the paper is part of my morning ritual. I grew up reading a daily newspaper – both my parents read the paper when I was a kid and they still do – so it's something I'm really comfortable doing – but I'm shocked that so many of my friends and clients don't read newspapers anymore.

While media savvy interviewees said their choice of a primary news outlet helped them to deal with the issue of fake news, 41 interviewees said they often found it difficult to determine what was real and what was fake news. This was particularly the case for interviewees who got their news from social media and from television. Tony, a 23-year-old maintenance worker from Portland, Oregon, got all his news from Twitter. While he followed a couple of publications on the platform, he preferred to read the Tweets that other people posted in response to new stories. As Tony explained:

I guess I don't care that much about news. I work hard and Twitter's fun. I guess I could read more stories myself but they're often dull and dry. But other people's Tweets about the stories are much, much more entertaining and often make me laugh, particularly when they say outrageous things. I've even repeated some of the Tweets in conversations with friends but then when I think about it I wonder if I'm actually spreading fake news.

Brenda, a 55-year-old nurse from Oklahoma, received all her news from television and found it difficult to fact-check broadcast news claims:

I'm a big TV watcher, I have it on all the time I'm home. I watch "Good Morning America" each day as I get ready for work and I usually have the local or national news on when I get home after work. I like the news segments on "Good Morning America," especially when they're upbeat stories about working people. But I don't like some of the nightly news, about jobs and the economy and health care and the military and I don't know who they're relying on for their information. How do you know if the stories are real? How can you check? I know that newspapers often list their sources but I really don't have the time to read newspapers anymore.

Similarly, Toby, a 42-year-old construction worker from Green Bay, Wisconsin, got his news from television and from Facebook. As Toby said:

I'm a huge Packers fan and my local broadcast station has solid coverage about them, their games, and their fans and even some interesting information about baseball and college sports. I also get lots of news in my Facebook feed. I'm pretty confident with the sports coverage – especially about the Pack and the Brewers but sometimes I wonder how reliable the national news really is. I've heard people say it's fake news and I wonder if maybe some of it is.

Other interviewees said they did not have a regular news source. A few people said they did not follow the news because it was "too political," "all propaganda" or "full of conflict," and a few individuals insisted that the news was "irrelevant" to their lives. Others did not follow a main news source but they accessed news from aggregators like the *Huffington Post*, the *Daily Beast* or *Reddit*. Melissa, a 25-year-old graduate student from Philadelphia, got all her news from *The Skimm*, an aggregator targeted to female millennials:

I get *The Skimm* in my Facebook feed each morning. They have easy-to-read news stories that I can get through fast and I feel good knowing what's going on each day. But recently at school some other graduate students were discussing some big foreign news story that I knew nothing about. I kept quiet because I was a little uncomfortable knowing nothing about it. I guess it was an important story. And so I started wondering if maybe I wasn't getting all the news I needed. Maybe *The Skimm* is just giving me what I want to read – but is it all real news and if it is, I wonder if that's enough?

4 Coexisting technologies

Diverse media

Much of the research regarding the use of digital technologies has been based on an assumption that the development of each new technique, technology or artifact destroyed the viability of the previous one. Known as the "doctrine of supersession" (Eisenstein 1997, p. 1054), this perspective considered it imperative for people to embrace technological developments so that they were not left behind. However, contemporary research on the utilization of new media as well as insights from the individuals I interviewed did not support a doctrine of supersession, but instead illustrated the coexistence of diverse media artifacts, styles and technologies (Eisenstein 1997). All 105 interviewees consciously and actively made choices about which technologies they used and which ones they rejected. When new technologies fit with their needs and interests, some interviewees happily incorporated them into the routines of their daily lives. However, other individuals were extremely cautious about adding any digital technologies to their current practices. People's reasons for opting in and opting out of digital media were complex and multidimensional, but most interviewees said they were comfortable mixing new technologies with older ones.

This chapter addresses the current trend of mixing analog with digital media technologies. Specifically, it discusses the popularity of "older" technologies like record albums, commonly known as vinyl, paper books, magazines and newspapers as well as the use of typewriters and film-based cameras and considers how people integrate these analog technologies with digital technologies and tools.

Paper books

Throughout this research project, one older technology emerged in interviews as the single most preferred technology – books on paper.

While it was rare for all interviewees to agree on one perspective, approach or use of technology, when it came to reading paper books, all 105 interviewees said that whenever possible they preferred to read hardcover or paperback books. Many of the interviewees also read books on their tablets, Kindles or iPads, and some read PDFs on their smartphones or computers at work or while traveling. However, interviewees repeatedly explained that it was not their reading tool of choice and that they only used digital options when they needed to do so. Several people said they found it difficult to read digital books; they mentioned having vision problems and noted that they often had trouble keeping their place on their digital readers. Others said that they found it difficult to remember what they previously read on digital devices and said they were frequently frustrated when the batteries on their devices died and they ran out of power.

Yet, all interviewees found paper books "indispensable," "awesome" or "one of my favorite things." They spoke of their love of "the touch, the feel and the smell of books" and noted that it was the "physical weight of a book" that made them feel "comfortable," "calm," "engaged," "happy" and/or "complete." Undergraduate and graduate students alike felt that reading paper books for their classes helped them focus better and retain more information, and several students noted that they enjoyed having something concrete to hold on to while they were studying. More than half of the people I interviewed said that reading paper books was their "favorite leisure activity." Some people differentiated between reading for work or school and reading for pleasure. For example, Benji, a 29-year-old graduate student from Atlanta, Georgia, explained: "If it's leisure reading, if it's pleasure reading, if it's anything for me, I like feeling the pages." Benji said that he resisted e-book readers because:

> I don't want to read something at length on a screen. Not only do I have the sense that I don't fully own this – it isn't something I can hold in my hands but I don't get the experience of reading a book…I don't really interact with it beyond the screen.

Interviewees' commentary supported current research that people who read paper books considered them "more satisfying" and less distracting than digital readers. Researchers have found that when people read paper books, their "minds process abstract information more effectively" (Friedman 2018, p. 104) and that paper books engaged readers' senses: "from the smell of the paper and glue to the sight of the cover design and weight of the pages read, and the sound of those sheets turning, and even the subtle taste of the ink on your fingertips" (Sax 2017).

Comments from interviewees corresponded with the current resurgence of printed books in the U.S. According to a 2016 Pew Research Center study, 65 percent of adult Americans had read a printed book during the last year (Victor 2016). In addition, the Association of American Publishers recently reported that books on paper continued their growth trend from 2017. For the first quarter of 2018, print book revenue in the U.S. was $1.14 billion, which was up about $67.7 million from the same period in 2017. Sales of hardback books were up 12 percent while paperback book sales were up 3.2 percent (Book Publisher Revenue, 2018).

Journals and writing implements

Thirty of the people I interviewed regularly read print magazines and 25 individuals said they read print copies of a newspaper on a weekly basis. Karen, a 48-year-old accountant from Ventura, California, was one of 15 interviewees who kept a paper journal and said she considered it a more creative medium than any digital technology. She used digital technologies at work and owned a smartphone, but she preferred using blank bound books for her creative endeavors. She filled her bound books with poems, drawings, photographs and inspiring quotations. Other interviewees spoke of using legal pads, spiral notebooks and bound journals in their leisure time, while some routinely used bound journals for brainstorming work projects. These interviewees said that their paper journals gave them more freedom to be creative. Their views aligned with those of David Sax (2017), author of *The Revenge of Analog: Real Things and Why They Matter*, who has maintained that while a piece of paper has a fixed size and is limited by marks made on it, its simplicity also offered "a powerful efficiency." Sax explained that with pen and paper a person "is free to write, doodle or scribble her idea however she wishes between those borders, without the restrictions or distractions imposed by software."

All 15 interviewees who said they kept some type of paper journal discussed their preferences for specific writing implements. Some interviewees said they had extensive collections of pens, markers and pencils, while others only kept a few choice pens that they used to sign important documents or create special projects. Two interviewees preferred to use number two pencils that they liked to be sharpened to a "perfect point." A few interviewees differentiated between functional writing implements that they use for everyday tasks and special pens that they used when they wanted to express themselves creatively.

Several interviewees noted that using older writing implements like fountain pens was a specific way they distinguished themselves from others. As Barbie, a 41-year-old lawyer from Orange County, California, commented:

> I have a nice collection of pens and pencils. I use most of them, like my gel pens, markers, felt tips and mechanical pencils, for everyday stuff like making lists and notes. But when I'm writing in my journal or sending a personal letter, I like to use one of my fountain pens. I have three of them – they're sleek and elegant and I love how they feel in my hand. My writing looks and feels special when I use one of them.

Barbie said that all three of her fountain pens have special meaning to her. She received a Montblanc pen from her parents when she passed the bar and she found the other two fountain pens at antique shops in San Francisco. Upon reflection, Barbie said that "For me, using one of my fountain pens is an important part of my identity. I like to be known as a lawyer who writes with a fountain pen – I think it distinguishes me, makes me a little unique."

Andy, a 24-year-old business graduate student from Philadelphia, Pennsylvania, also mentioned his pen collection during his interview. Andy said that while his collection was modest, it included two fountain pens that he had inherited from his grandfather:

> I love all kinds of pens and like to use really narrow felt tips to take notes in my classes and of course I always use markers and highlighters when reading and studying. But my grandpa left me his two special fountain pens when he passed and I've started really getting into them and learning more about special ink and paper for them. The pens are sterling silver and they're pretty old – I think they first belonged to my grandpa's father.

Andy said he has developed a special interest in fountain pen ink because he found it:

> beautiful to look at. There are variations in the color and it's so different than the ink for other pens. When you use nice ink, the pens just seem to float over the paper – it's makes writing a different experience.

Interviewees like Barbie and Andy represented the emergence of a new popular culture trend. According to a December 2018 article in *The New*

York Times, old-fashioned writing implements like the fountain pen are making a comeback. "Twenty-first century pen nerds" are collecting fountain pens, ink and specialized papers. While some "pen nerds" are artists, collectors and writers, many pen enthusiasts "are administrative professionals who just have normal cubicle office jobs, and they just want interesting tools to make their day more their own" (Purves 2018).

Instant cameras and flip phones

Sales of instant film cameras and flip phones are also increasing in the U.S. Polaroid, best known for its self-developing film, nearly went bankrupt at the beginning of the twenty-first century. Now, it is a hot commodity, with its cameras and film selling out swiftly. In order to keep up with consumer demand, Polaroid recently sought out old cameras that could be refurbished. While Hollywood celebrities who have been worried about cyberspace hacking have promoted the use of Polaroids, people of all ages have been enjoying the instant film cameras. During her interview, Karen said that she had recently started taking Polaroids and enjoyed adding them to her bound books: "I love the idea of artist books and I've been combining Polaroids with my poems and drawings. I'm not there yet but my goal is to create an artist book of my own." According to Creed O'Hanlon, chief executive of Polaroid, in the last few years, teenagers have been buying most of the instant film cameras. O'Hanlon said that teens particularly enjoyed taking a picture and "seeing an image slowly appear in the palm of their hand. People love the tangibility. You can write on it, you can give it to somebody. It feels one-off and more special than just transferring you a file" (quoted in Langley 2015).

Basic flip phones like Jitterbug and Jethrow have been marketed to senior citizens because they were sturdy, simple to use and were only used to make and receive calls. During my interview with Ruth, an 81-year-old who lived in Southern California, she said that she owned a flip phone so that she would never have to text. Ruth considered herself knowledgeable about digital technologies and said that she regularly emailed friends and family members and was on social media each day. However, she disliked texting because she thought it was a terrible communication medium.

As Ruth explained:

> I want to see their faces when I talk with my family and friends. If I can't be with them in person, I want to hear their voices, connect with them, not merely see the top of their heads and share texts with them. I want to know what they are thinking, what they are

feeling, if they are doing well, if they need anything from me. You can't get any real conversation going through texts. You just share superficial silly comments.

Ruth recounted a recent trip she took to Chicago where she observed most of the people on the flight engaging solely with their screens and said she felt uncomfortable about what she saw: "The airplane was so quiet. No one was talking. Everyone was looking at their phones, their iPads, their Kindles or their laptops. No one was interacting and no one was communicating. It's sad." Ruth saw her refusal to text as a way of being true to herself and asserting her authority over new technologies. She explained that while she enjoyed keeping up with friends on Facebook and email, she wanted to maintain face-to-face communication with her family whenever possible.

Flip phones have also become popular with celebrities, teens and others who want to connect in more traditional ways. In addition to their simplicity, users have found them less distracting and more convenient to use. Flip phones are less expensive than smartphones, have a longer battery life, are more durable and have better call quality. In addition, they offer greater security because they cannot be hacked and cannot share personal information (Miller 2015). Privacy issues and security problems connected with digital technologies were of fundamental importance to many interviewees, and their concerns have been addressed more fully in Chapter 6. However, several interviewees discussed their decision to give up their smartphones for flip phones and agreed with a 30-year-old technology analyst from Washington D.C. John that constant connectivity encouraged data hacking and compromised individuals' personal security. As John explained:

> I switched to a flip phone several years ago so that I wouldn't be connected all the time and my data would be more secure. With the Internet of Things, I'm concerned about the privacy of my information – particularly the data that I don't want to share. So many digital things are now connected and that connectivity makes hacking and data breaches so much easier. So many people have the illusion that their information is safe – it really isn't that safe so it's important to take steps to protect it.

The typewriter

Intelligence agents, politicians, writers and movie stars have embraced yet another analog technology – the manual typewriter. There is currently a typewriter museum, a typewriter orchestra, public type-ins, a Facebook page, a Twitter hashtag (#typewritercollector) and the blog typosphere (typosphere.blogspot.com) for people who are obsessed with typewriters and other "obsolete technologies," including handwriting, paper mail, pens and ink and film photography. According to Richard Polt, author of *Typewriter Revolution*, while typewriters previously represented technological efficiency and standardization, the contemporary use of this analog machine has helped people to distance themselves from contemporary digital technologies (Lange 2017). In the 2017 documentary, *California Typewriter*, director/photographer/editor Doug Nichol offered a pointed critique of the digital age and suggested that in an effort to make life easier, new technologies have taken us away from an authentic reality. Nichol's focus on the physicality of the typewriter and its function as a writing tool addressed its role as a "totem of the twentieth-century mind" (Gleiberman 2017).

The documentary included commentary from typewriter devotees like actor Tom Hanks, who considered himself obsessive about typewriters. Hanks owns hundreds of vintage machines and uses them to communicate with fans, friends and family members. Hanks found typewriters "reassuring, comforting, dazzling in that here is a very specific apparatus that is meant to do one thing, and it does it perfectly." For Hanks, typewriters did a great job translating the thoughts in our minds to paper and he maintained that "short of carving words into stone with a hammer and chisel, not much is more permanent than a paragraph or a sentence or a love letter or a story typed on paper" (quoted in Greene 2017). According to the documentary, before his death, Pulitzer Prize-winning author/actor Sam Shepard preferred to write on a typewriter because he said he never felt comfortable writing on a computer. Shepard noted that his use of a typewriter placed him in a different relationship with contemporary society, but he felt that because the computer screen was "removed from tactile experience" he chose the typewriter. As Shepard explained: "When you go to ride a horse, you have to saddle it. When you use a typewriter, you have to feed it paper. There's a percussion about it. You can see the ink flying onto the surface of the paper" (quoted in Gleiberman 2017).

During my interview with Mike, a 31-year-old writer from Brooklyn, New York, he said that he preferred to use his Underwood typewriter for all his creative writing activities. While Mike wrote freelance articles on his laptop, he felt that his computer actually stifled his creativity: "On my typewriter, I can feel myself writing – I hear the sounds of the keys and I know I'm writing. I like the feel of the machine and

I stay focused and I concentrate much better on my Underwood." Mike added that when he wrote on a computer he found it difficult to concentrate solely on his writing because "I'm always checking my Twitter or email."

While Mike and Karen differentiated between their work and their creative writing, none of my student interviewees commented on using different writing tools for different types of writing. All graduate and undergraduate students said they relied on their laptops for all of their school work as well as any creative writing or design work that they did. Several students mentioned that they liked the convenience of having all their assignments easily accessible and they found their laptops an invaluable resource for revising and editing their work.

The resurgence of vinyl

Although analog technologies are often bulkier and costlier than their digital counterparts, many older technologies are thought to offer "a richness of experience that is unparalleled with anything delivered through a screen" (Sax 2017). Certainly, the growth of vinyl records supported this view as well as reinforced the perspective of diverse media technologies coexisting with each other. During most of the twentieth century, vinyl records were the most popular medium for the reproduction of commercial music. While early vinyl recordings were produced in a variety of speeds and sizes, after World War II, the long play 33 RPM album dominated the music industry. However, by the late 1980s, the development of the digital compact disk (CD) overtook vinyl as the primary carrier of music ('A Short History' 2018) and most technology insiders began to see vinyl albums as "an endangered species." Yet, vinyl survived the 1990s, in part because disk jockeys preferred it and it retained its relevance in music genres like techno, hip hop, reggae and house. By 2010, when playing MP3 files on an iPod was the most popular choice for listening to commercial music, vinyl had become the fastest growing music format (Bartmanski and Woodward 2015).

In an effort to promote new interest in vinyl albums, a group of independent record store owners began a yearly Record Store Day in 2007. The event is currently celebrated internationally each April; it includes many genres of music and features special releases from both mainstream and independent artists. Vinyl is now sold in the U.S. by a variety of retail outlets, including Amazon, Barnes & Noble and Urban Outfitters, and vinyl subscription services offer users a mixture of old and new releases as well as music rarities and unreleased items.

For example, each month Vnyl subscribers receive records geared to their specific musical tastes, while Vinyl Me, Please sends subscribers a handpicked record paired with a piece of art and a recipe for a custom cocktail (Ediriwira 2016).

During the last decade, vinyl sales in the U.S. increased more than 1,000 percent, from 1 million albums sold in 2007 to 14.3 million albums sold in 2017 (Richter 2018). Sales during the first half of 2018 were up 19.2 percent over 2017 and vinyl album sales represented more than 18 percent of all new album sales (Helfet 2018). Yet, these statistics only addressed new music sales; a considerable number of used record albums are sold at independent record stores, garage sales and through online venues. Some vinyl records have been released by contemporary musicians working in alternative rock, rhythm and blues, jazz, gospel, soundtracks, opera and classical music, while other vinyl recordings have been special releases of older albums. For example, the top selling vinyl LP for 2017 was a 50th anniversary reissue of The Beatles' "Sergeant Pepper's Lonely Hearts Club Band," which was first released on May 26, 1967. In addition, special vinyl releases for 2018 included reissues of Bruce Springsteen, Prince, Ella Fitzgerald and a soundtrack of two "Doctor Who" stories (Caulfield 2018).

Researchers have studied vinyl users, offering their experiences to illustrate the interests of people who willingly unplugged from digital technologies and embraced analog technology. Thoren and colleagues (2017) suggested that vinyl users developed a bond to the physical vinyl artifacts and that they enjoyed the focused listening and the way it signaled users' individuality. These researchers used the term "hipster," which they defined as a nonconformist subculture representing individuals "who actively and with some discerning tastes seek out the alternative route of deliberate disconnect" (p. 2) as a framework through which to understand why vinyl users chose not to engage with digital music. Similarly, Bartmanski and Woodward (2015) found that vinyl's popularity, in spite of its cost and lack of portability, illustrated its authenticity as a music medium. They suggested that the attention required by listeners to care for the vinyl and manually turn over each record at the end of a side encouraged people "to ritualize and celebrate the act of listening" (p. 8).

The humanity and authenticity of vinyl was also addressed by Yochim and Biddinger (2005), particularly as it related to listeners asserting their need for authentic human connections by choosing to listen to music through the physical analog technology. Other researchers have maintained that some people embraced older analog technologies as a sign of resistance to being sold more complex and expensive solutions to nonexistent problems, while other individuals chose older technologies because they wanted to slow down and no longer wished to be rushed. (Langley 2015). Many sound professionals, DJs and music fans considered sound quality the most compelling reason for their vinyl preference. Some devotees suggested that vinyl was a more authentic technology that showcased the human touch in its recordings, while others maintained that vinyl record albums produced a deeper bass and a more expansive frequency range that was closer to the original harmonic structure of the music. However, other music critics have suggested that the current interest in vinyl was merely a case of musical nostalgia. Considering the trend misplaced, they have called the analog technology bulky, inefficient or even the result of a Luddite mentality.

Vinyl collections

Music technology was a topic that elicited strong opinions from many of the people I interviewed. Several interviewees streamed music through Spotify and Pandora and some preferred Apple Music, while others listened to their favorite music on their phones, iPods, laptops and tablets. Some interviewees still had large CD collections and others preferred to listen to music on Sirius XM Satellite radio or on their favorite local FM radio station. A few individuals played musical instruments, but they did not listen to any music through digital or analog services or devices and one third of the interviewees preferred vinyl over any digital technology. Most of these individuals described themselves as tech savvy and said they were passionate about vinyl as the consummate music medium. While media and researchers have used the term hipsters to define vinyl devotees, none of the people I interviewed referred to themselves as hipsters.

Vinyl aficionados frequently discussed how they began their album collections. For example, Rick, a nonprofit communication specialist from Tennessee, used to listen to music on his iPhone but started to collect vinyl a few years ago because of its artwork. He would go into used record stores and said that he "loved the ephemera, the album artwork, the knowledge. I liked the idea of looking at a complete idea of what it was." Rick explained that when he purchased an album he found it a completely different experience than streaming music or buying an audio file: "It's the idea of an album that you're buying more than just the music itself. You're buying an experience or looking at the artwork, looking at the information and reading the lyrics. I find that more immersive." Several other interviewees agreed with Rick's views regarding the artwork on the album covers and record sleeves and said that they felt the liner notes provided listeners with key information about the music and was an important feature that was missing with digital music.

After Rick began collecting vinyl, he said he would always check out the Goodwill bin and that family members and friends would bring him crates full of their old albums. While many of the albums were not to his musical taste, he kept some of them because of their "weird" art. Rick said he soon began becoming more professional about his vinyl collection:

> because I love classic soul and Isaac Hayes and so I started going to more specialty stores and vinyl shops. It's a great experience searching for albums and I enjoy the ritual of listening to this music much more than listening on my MP3 player.

Cheryl, a 66-year-old teacher from Minneapolis, began buying record albums as a teenager and never switched to using any digital music technology. She said that she currently has thousands of albums in her collection. While many of her albums were purchased new, throughout the years she has also shopped at secondhand stores and garage sales for used record albums to replace damaged recordings and to add interesting new records to her collection. "I've gotten some really awesome finds at garage sales – used albums but in great shape – that you can't get elsewhere – or if you can they're a lot more expensive." Cheryl was proud of her record collection and said:

> My record albums are really important to me. One of my first albums was Simon and Garfunkel's "Sounds of Silence," which I still love and listen to – even though it's scratched and a little warped now. I've always enjoyed their harmonies and their lyrics are the best poetry. My daughter recently played a few songs from it for me on Apple Music and it just wasn't the same. The songs were flat, less emotional and it reminded me how lucky I am to have saved all my albums.

Like Cheryl, several other interviewees compared the sound quality of digital music with vinyl recordings and some mentioned that they had recently turned to vinyl because they found that electronic music had become "repetitive," "sanitized" or "too tame" for them. According to a *Wired* music critic, digital recordings are composed from strings of ones and zeros, which result in a specific tone and style with a distinct beginning and end, while analog recordings provide additional nuance and depth and allow music sounds to fade naturally (Krummenacher 2012).

It was the sound particularly the popping and crackling noises that Warren, a 39-year-old mechanic from Atlanta, Georgia, said helped him to distinguish the authenticity of vinyl records from any digital music:

> When I'm listening to an album from the 1960s, like say Marvin Gay's "I Heard it Through the Grapevine," the sounds the vinyl makes help the rhythm of the music – and makes it richer, more real. The album is old and when I put it on the turntable it sounds sorta old which is fine because it is. When I hear digital recordings, even when they're of older music, they always sound new to me but not new in a good way – somehow all digital music sounds the same – kind of like elevator music.

All interviewees who preferred vinyl insisted that the sound was "better," "more authentic," "more real" or of "higher quality" than digital music. Interviewees found the listening experience more like "hearing live music" and said that when listening to vinyl they heard the story coming through the album and were able to "let the music wash over them." Several people had harsh criticism for digital music calling it "fake music," "artificial," "meaningless," "manufactured solely for profit," "soulless" or "insignificant." In each case, sound quality was far more important than any physical inconvenience or additional costs involved with collecting vinyl.

Vinyl's physicality

In addition to the sound quality, interviewees also mentioned the physicality of vinyl records. In their interviews, they discussed the care they took with their albums and the need to get up and turn each record over, as well as the weight of the album in their hands and the technique needed to carefully place the needle on the record album. Mitch, a 22-year-old music lover from Denver, Colorado, said that he particularly enjoyed the physical aspects of owning record albums:

> I felt a very strong physical and tactile sense with it that I really enjoyed. I loved the fact that halfway through I would have to flip it and it really transformed what had previously been background listening for me and into something that was very ritualistic. I listen to a lot of music to try to relax. Listening to albums was almost meditative – even simply watching the revolution of the

album pleased me. I loved the sound of it as well. So much richer, real and authentic than digital downloads.

Similarly, Mary, a 32-year-old bartender from Trenton, New Jersey, suggested that the effort vinyl requires is to her an important aspect of its appeal:

> Listening to vinyl requires a commitment to the music, an amount of dedication that's more than just playing tunes. You need to really listen to the music, take care of the albums and stay in one place to hear the music. To me, playing an album on my turntable is an event – it's something quite special to me.

Mary considered vinyl a more human technology and said that several of her friends regularly got together to listen to music and play their newly acquired albums.

Other interviewees mentioned what they called the culture of vinyl, specifically how they viewed it a technology that could bring people together. For example, Vicky, a 64-year-old grandmother from Toledo, Ohio, said that when her family got together during holidays they enjoyed listening to music together:

> My husband and I have been collecting albums since we were teenagers and we've never listened to anything else. We have a great collection of 60s and 70s folk music and rock and roll – psychedelic rock too – that my children discovered when they became teenagers. I'll never forget the time when my daughter discovered our "American Beauty" album by the Dead – her mind was blown.

Both of Vicky's children began collecting record albums in college and have shared their favorite music with her ever since. Vicky began playing her folk albums for her grandchildren when they were toddlers "and they loved it and soon they were asking to play music every time we got together." Vicky said that now everyone in her family collects vinyl and shares music with other members of the family:

> One of our longstanding holiday traditions is for each person to bring an album to share. We set aside time to listen and it's a great time for all of us to learn about new singers and bands and to share our love of music with the others.

Both Mitch and Mary were also introduced to vinyl albums by their parents and said that they received their first turntables as holiday gifts. Mary often shopped for record albums with her father and Mitch noted that he enjoyed introducing his family to music he liked. As Mitch explained:

> After listening to lots of my parents' albums – and borrowing many of them – I have a sense of their taste in tunes, and now it's fun to expose them to other types of music – especially to new and upcoming artists. Collecting vinyl is something we have in common – it's something we love to talk about and do together.

The identity of vinyl

These days, due to file sharing and streaming services, many people's digital music collections are quite similar. Yet, collecting vinyl and showcasing a different range of music was a way that interviewees said they exerted their independence and authority over digital technology. It also helped them to set themselves apart from others and helped them to become known as authentic music fans. According to Bill Gagnon, a senior vice president in charge of vinyl releases at EMI Catalog Marketing, people who bought vinyl identified with the "earthy authenticity" of the format. They also viewed their use of vinyl as central to their persona. Gagnon saw the adoption of vinyl as a "back-to nature approach," and suggested: "It's the difference between growing your own vegetables and purchasing them frozen in the supermarket" (quoted in Williams 2008).

This perspective clearly resonated with the interviewees who chose to listen to record albums rather than to embrace digital music. While vinyl users were often quite knowledgeable about new media and used digital technologies in other aspects of their lives, they frequently described their rejection of digital music technologies as an integral part of their identities. Being a vinyl devotee was a significant way that interviewees defined themselves, saw themselves and represented themselves to others. Several interviewees said that their use of vinyl highlighted their interpersonal interactions and offered a "shorthand representation" of who they were.

As Alexis, a 24-year-old barista from Portland, Oregon, noted:

> With vinyl I am very aware of the fact that it takes effort putting it on the turntable, placing the needle on it. I feel a very strong physical and tactile sense with it that I really enjoy. I love the fact that

halfway through I have to flip it. It's something I do because that's who I am. I collect vinyl – that's how I identify myself.

Several interviewees who preferred vinyl said that when they met a new person and learned that person had a turntable they felt "an immediate kinship" with that person because he or she "spoke the language of vinyl." Conversely, a few interviewees said that they had rejected dating people who only listened to digital music because they felt that they would not understand the role vinyl played in their lives and assumed that the person would not share their values or priorities. As Alexis explained:

I'm way more comfortable being with other vinyl collectors – without understanding my passion, how could they really know me? Maybe I'm being superficial but if you aren't a vinyl user, you don't really understand music – you're not really a real music lover.

5   The culture of opting out

Media resisters

Much of the technology resistance research has showcased individuals' conscious rejection of one or more digital technologies as being politically or culturally motivated action. People who opted out of new media were thought to be actively resisting consumer culture by participating in what Portwood-Stacer (2012) has called "conspicuous non-consumption" (p. 1047). These acts of resistance could be individual or part of a collective dissent movement. For Portwood-Stacer, "media refusal is a way of making one's everyday lifestyle into a site of resistance against the powerful, normative force of media consumer culture" (p. 1053). In an effort to slow down, disrupt or withdraw from online environments and platforms that they saw as having objectionable policies or practices, researchers have suggested that media resisters used several disruption strategies and techniques. Resisters made up fake social media profiles and shared grocery loyalty cards, in an attempt to make data gathering less reliable. They also slowed down platforms and systems by developing critical websites and disrupting the technological infrastructure. In addition, media resisters also withdrew from platforms and online sites that they believed were deceptive or encouraged passive participation.

Yet, none of the 105 people I interviewed for this project explicitly referred to themselves as media resisters, and no one described any strategies or techniques that they used to disrupt digital technology platforms. However, several interviewees said that they restricted their use of digital media because it did not fit with their cultural and/or ethical values, while others noted that they did not engage with new technology because it contradicted their political views or their religious values. In addition, many interviewees said that they felt the long-term influence that digital technologies might have on their families, communities, and culture would always need to be balanced against any individual person's desire to engage with new technology. Specifically, this chapter focuses on ethical, cultural, political and religious values and concerns related to interviewees' use and nonuse of digital technologies.

Intentional communities

Intentional communities built around communal spaces and gardens, common areas and facilities have become increasingly popular throughout the U.S. Thought to encourage a greater sense of community connection, some intentional communities are focused on common spiritual, environmental or political values while other communities are intergenerational, built to help alleviate loneliness and encourage the development of interpersonal relationships.

As a member of an intentional community in the small town of Viroqua, Wisconsin, 42-year-old Lars limited his use of digital technologies in order to become more focused on his community and to further develop his relationships with family and friends. Lars relied on a smartphone during his work as a professional salesman, but said that he preferred to use a landline for his home life and during other times that he planned "to initiate any kind of deep or personal conversation." Throughout his interview, Lars expressed his concerns about the millions of people who he described as "continually staring at their cell phones," and he said that he believed the use of digital technologies had "gone past utility into some addictive, weird, anti-social strange thing." Lars rejected all social media and called Twitter the "silliest of them" because it required users to "squish your message down to like a fragment for no good reason." Lars's wife did not own a cell phone and his family has never watched television. However, his 12-year-old son was allowed to play video games for one hour each day on an old Mac laptop. His son was also able to listen to an iPod Touch, which Lars considered "the gateway drug of the technology thing."

According to Lars, Viroqua residents saw themselves as part of a back-to-the-land cultural movement, and they wanted to have a greater influence over their children's education than was possible in other Wisconsin public schools. Community members developed a system of schooling based on the Waldorf educational philosophy of Rudolf Steiner. The Waldorf system was framed around the creation of an organic culture built in a natural setting that integrated intellectual learning and emotional character building with practical physical labor. Lars explained that the Viroqua school curriculum was based on a mindfulness doctrine; students were taught to meditate each morning and they routinely built things, played musical instruments and were encouraged to explore their environment each day. Lars described himself as "the most anti-technology person" on the school board and noted that at his direction the school had worked "to eliminate devices from all classrooms."

Technology and simple living

While the development of a Waldorf educational philosophy in their school was a key focus of the Viroqua community, other intentional communities have supported a wide variety of different initiatives based on values such as self-sufficiency, interpersonal development and voluntary simplicity. Two of the people I interviewed mentioned that their rationale for opting out of most digital technology was based on their personal philosophy of voluntary simplicity or simple living. Voluntary simplicity "rejects the high-consumption, materialistic lifestyles of consumer cultures" ("What is Voluntary Simplicity?" 2018) in favor of a meaningful life based on family, community, spiritual contemplation and a sense of responsibility about the ethical use of natural resources. Based on an assumption that people can live meaningful lives while consuming an equitable and sustainable share of the world's natural resources, voluntary simplicity is not anti-technology but it takes a critical stance on the benefits of new technologies, evaluating the costs and benefits to individuals, communities, the environment and to humanity.

Community unity was a central focus of interviewees' philosophy of simple living. George, a 51-year-old organic farmer from Northern California, said he mixed older farming techniques with newer technologies in an attempt to preserve the land for future generations. "We plant pest-resistant plants like peppermint and spearmint with our crops and try to provide a habitat that attracts helpful insects so that we don't need to use any pesticides that pollute the water or the land." George said that in examining his relationships with material possessions, money and the environment, he has:

> learned that happiness isn't really about owning things. You know the saying, "he who dies with the most toys, wins" – that's a lie – it isn't true. Fulfillment isn't about more – it's about better – what's better for us, for our families and for our planet.

Limiting his carbon footprint was extremely important to George, who said that he was concerned about the planned obsolescence within the technology industry. Planned obsolescence is a policy of planning and designing technologies and products with "an artificially limited useful life" (Sarhan 2017), so that they become less functional and consumers are regularly pressured into upgrading or buy new devices. George managed key aspects of his farm through his computer, but he did not use a smartphone because he felt that "the constant release of new and better and more expensive smartphones strikes me as wasteful and deceptive. I wonder how many older smartphones are now in landfills leaching harmful chemicals into the soil?"

Similarly, Tiffany, a 36-year-old nurse from Toledo, Ohio, who also practiced voluntary simplicity focused on community unity. During her interview, Tiffany said that she worried about the never-ending cycle of conspicuous consumption and maintained that "things don't bring you happiness – being a part of a community is what does." Tiffany used a variety of digital technologies at work but chose to live simply in her home life. "Rather than collecting stuff, I spend my free time and money traveling, meeting people from different countries and backgrounds and learning about new cultures." Like George, Tiffany also worried about planned obsolescence and mentioned that she was concerned about her sister because she was always upgrading her iPhone:

> My sister is constantly buying a new iPhone. Last year I suggested that we go on a trip together but she told me that she needed to save her money for a new iPhone. I told her she was wasting her life and her money but she said she needed the phone to stay in touch with her friends.

Tiffany does not own a personal computer or a smartphone and said that the only time she accessed her email was at work. She said that owning digital technologies would contradict her desire to live simply and added: "I don't need a home computer because I don't shop online and I have a (landline) telephone at home."

Environmental concerns

Neither George nor Tiffany referred to their anti-consumption behavior as being politically motivated and neither saw their actions regarding their technology use as any type of resistance. However, they both felt that their voluntary simplicity and their critical stance toward digital technologies were key components of their personal identity. George said that as a farmer, he saw himself as a "caretaker for nature. It's important for me to encourage Americans to make sure our oceans, lakes and rivers aren't polluted and that discarded plastic and metal from all of our screens doesn't clog our landfills." Protecting natural resources was George's mission, and he maintained that his identity was built on that mission. Similarly, Tiffany said that she identified as a person who was "opposed to excessive consumption of all things including new technology. I'm trying to lessen my carbon footprint and living simply makes sense to me. It's one of my core values."

While only George and Tiffany tied their views on digital technology use to their voluntary simplicity, 35 additional interviewees reported being concerned about the never-ending developments associated with digital technologies, particularly as they related to issues of consumption and planned obsolescence. Several interviewees echoed Tiffany's concerns about the continuous need to upgrade or buy new smartphones, while other interviewees felt that all the changes with computers during the last decade had increased their worries about planned obsolescence.

As Brent, a 49-year-old attorney from Flagstaff, Arizona, explained:

> Not only have laptops and operating systems changed, but now you can't even use the same plugs and adaptors anymore. Talk about a waste – I have boxes full of this stuff, external disk drives, connectors, thumb drives – none of them work on my computer without me buying yet another adaptor. And don't get me started on CDs – my current laptop doesn't even have a CD drive – so everything I've saved over the years isn't easily accessible – if this isn't planned obsolescence, I don't know what is.

Many of the interviewees who said they were concerned about planned obsolescence and overconsumption connected their views about their digital technology usage with their personal views on the environment. Interviewees of all ages were concerned with the amount of waste being dumped in landfills and how that waste impacted the overall health of the earth. Ten interviewees said that they had become more politically active because of a general lack of concern among political leaders about key environmental problems. They said it was through their political activity that they became more aware of the negative influence of digital technologies on our environment. Their views echoed recent findings regarding the influence of discarded electronics, also known as technotrash, on the environment. According to the Digital Responsibility organization, worldwide only about 25 percent of electronics are recycled and between 20 and 50 million tons of electronics are discarded into landfills each year. The technotrash in landfills includes a variety of heavy metals and toxic materials like mercury and lead that can seep into the ground water, affect wild animals, crops and plants and pollute the earth. On average, each computer and monitor utilizes more than 500 pounds of fossil fuel (Soltan 2018).

While environmentally conscious interviewees worried about tech-notrash, some people saw the development of computers as an example of how to limit wasteful consumption and as a fundamental component of their own environmental activism. As Jennifer, a 42-year-old teacher from Richmond, Virginia, explained:

> I'm very active online. I support a variety of environmental causes like conserving coral reefs, saving the polar bears and cleaning up ocean waste and I have signed many online petitions and emailed my political representatives to lobby for more sustainable environmental policies. I don't think I'd be as active without my computer – if I wasn't online.

In addition, some interviewees mentioned that social media has helped them to understand and support important environmental efforts. In a few cases, interviewees have raised money for specific environmental initiatives through Facebook.

Other interviewees discussed the positive impact that digital technology has had on trash generation and disposal and felt that when people acted responsibly, there was much less of a need for paper trash. The majority of interviewees in their 20s and 30s thought that the U.S. currently generated less paper waste because fewer businesses were sending direct mail solicitation, and many younger people now received e-bills rather than paper bills. They also said that recycling was encouraged in most cities and states.

Several of the undergraduate and graduate students I interviewed felt that their use of a computer had helped them to develop sustainable consumption practices. Paul, an undergraduate student from Chicago, discussed how he used his computer for class-related activities:

> All of my readings, assignments, notes and work are created and filed on my laptop. That way I don't lose anything. I rarely need to print anything out because my professors use drop box or allow us to email our assignments to them. That way less paper goes into landfills.

Paul mentioned a recent meeting with one of his professors at which he became dismayed by the stacks of printed paper in the professor's office.

He's old and I couldn't believe the mess. It looked like an episode of "Hoarders." He had stacks of books everywhere and piles of paper on his desk, covering his bookshelves – everywhere – even all over the floor. I wanted to tell him he was destroying the planet but I didn't want to be disrespectful. But really – someone needs to talk to him.

Cultural and religious identities

In contemporary American society, some individuals have restricted the use of digital technology because of their cultural and ethical values, while others considered technology as something that must be subsumed to their cultural and religious identities. Some spiritual leaders have raised concerns regarding the influence of new technologies on their parishioners and some religions have imposed strict policies about the role of technology in the lives of their congregations.

For example, the many groups of Plain People of North America deliberatively consider which technologies are appropriate for their communities and which technologies should be banned. Comprised of approximately 250 Old Order Amish and Mennonite settlements in 23 states, about 200,000 Plain People have resisted assimilation to mainstream American cultural values because they consider them a serious threat to their way of life. While some cultural practices among the settlements differ, all Plain People separate themselves from mainstream American culture by travelling by horse and carriage, wearing distinctive and plain clothing, speaking the Pennsylvania German Dialect and holding "strict taboos on television, radios, VCRs, and computers" (Kraybill 1998, p. 101). Emphasizing the collective good over individual wants or needs, the Plain People's culture focuses on core beliefs of humility, obedience, modesty, simplicity and submission to the will of God, which is known as Gelassenheit. "Whereas modern culture heralds individual achievement, advancement, and personal recognition, Gelassenheit calls for hesitating, slowing down, and backing off" (Kraybill 1998, p. 102).

The Plain People do not reject all new technologies, but they consider the long-term potential harm that the introduction of each new technology might have on their culture. Technologies that clash with Gelassenheit principles or that encourage luxury, vanity or sloth are banned; however, new technologies that enhance agricultural and economic productivity and fit within the community's regulations may be accepted. The Plain People use flashlights, generators, batteries, solar panels and water wheels to generate electricity and, while automobiles are forbidden because they are considered a status symbol that separates family,

Plain People rent busses, travel by train or fly when necessary (Kraybill 2001). Media and communication technologies are carefully screened and mostly restricted due to concerns about the influence of mainstream ideas on their culture. While televisions, radios, CDs, DVDs, VCRs and computers are forbidden in most settlements, word processors with small display screens, hand-held calculators, telephones and answering machines have been adapted or accepted (Cooper 2006).

Like the Plain People, the ultra-Orthodox (Haredi) Jews reject or avoid most new communication media because they fear that these technologies could threaten the ethical and religious values of their community. The Haredi adhere strictly to traditional Jewish laws and tend to distance themselves from the outside world, whereas other Orthodox Jewish groups interact with the modern world and tend to have more flexible views toward new technology. Ultra-Orthodox Jews do not watch television, movies or engage with popular culture; however, there is a growing trend toward using computers and the Internet for business purposes. The Internet is thought to present "significant socio-economic opportunities for the community and is seen as necessary for taking part in the changing job market" (Livio and Weinblatt 2007, p. 31). In addition, "Kosher phones" that allow users to make and receive calls but block text messaging and Internet access have been approved by Haredi leaders and are currently being used by community members.

In addition to ultra-Orthodox communities, many other religious Jews do not watch television, play video games or go to the movies because they find that many new technologies are distractions that are in conflict with their cultural and religious values. During her interview, Sarah, an Orthodox Jew in her 30s from New York, said that family members' decisions about which new technologies they used were based on their religious beliefs and values. As Sarah explained:

> Our family is observant but not Hasidic [ultra-Orthodox], yet we also believe that electronic devices are not conducive to our way of life. New technologies provide people with immediate gratification and their use encourages them to consume more and more material things. We do not want our children to be distracted by consuming things – we want them to use their minds and their imaginations to learn and to explore the world.

Sarah's four children attended a technology-free Jewish day school and the school has encouraged parents to forbid video games and to restrict their children's access to the Internet at home. While Sarah's husband used a computer with Internet access at work and owned a smartphone, the family did not have a personal computer or a television at home. Each member of Sarah's family played a musical instrument and Sarah said, "all of my children love to read and write."

The Church of Jesus Christ of Latter-Day Saints, commonly known as the Mormon church, also encourages its followers to be careful not to let digital technologies control them. Warning against using technology for inappropriate purposes, the church's "Safeguards for Using Technology" (2015) recommends to their missionaries that they should "choose wisely when using media because whatever you read, listen to, or look at has an effect on you. Select only media that uplifts you." Mormons are warned against using digital devices when they are alone and are encouraged to limit their technology usage when they are "feeling bored, lonely, angry, anxious, stressed or tired," because at those times they are considered vulnerable to the influence of unholy thoughts and ideas.

During his interview, Tim, a 24-year-old graduate student from Utah, said that his Mormon upbringing and his missionary experience has helped frame his views on digital technologies. While he regularly used digital technologies, he said he used them purposefully and in accordance with his religious training: "I access the Internet for my classes and write papers on my laptop. I also have a smartphone and I'm on Facebook and Twitter. But I mainly use social media and my smartphone to share scripture and help others." As a Mormon, Tim noted that he had been trained to "keep unholy thoughts from entering my mind and not to access anything violent, vulgar, immoral or pornographic on the Internet." Tim said that he considered his smartphone and iPad particularly useful in increasing the effectiveness of his missionary work because they helped him to easily access lessons and scripture. He also mentioned that during missionary training, filters had been installed on his smartphone "to help me focus on God's purpose and to protect me from inappropriate content." During his missionary training, Tim said that he was taught not to waste his time playing games, watching videos or accessing violent content.

Sheila, a 48-year-old office worker from a small town in Minnesota, also addressed the religious foundations for her views on technology. Calling herself a "previously lapsed but now serious Catholic," the mother of four was an early adopter of digital technology but now said she followed the teachings of Pope Francis and limited her children's screen time:

> When the kids were little we let them play video games all the time and they had full access to our home computer and the Internet. They were always online and my husband and I started to get worried about it.

Sheila said that she began to see less interaction between her children and thought that they were communicating less with each other:

> I looked up during one Sunday dinner, at the end of 2014 or maybe it was the beginning of 2015, where no one was talking and everyone was staring down, doing their own thing. My husband and my two older daughters were on their iPhones, my older son was on his iPad and the baby was playing a video game. That's when I said, "Enough is enough."

Searching for a solution for her concerns about digital technologies, Sheila said she remembered a World Communications Day talk by Pope Francis, during which he had warned about the need for families to talk with each other:

> My husband and I found the Pope's talk online and we watched it. His words helped us create a plan for our family. Pope Francis urged all Catholics to use technology wisely and not be overcome by it and he recommended that we cut down on screen time and put away our screens during meals.

Sheila said that now family dinners are screen free and that her children must complete their homework before they use any digital technologies for entertainment purposes. "My husband and I are online less now too and there's more talking at mealtimes – I'm thankful for the Pope's guidance on technology."

While many public and private schools have integrated digital technologies into all levels of their curriculum, some schools like the Viroqua school described by Lars, remain technology free due to curricular reasons. Yet other private schools have limited the use of digital technologies for religious and moral reasons and have developed technology policies in line with their moral and ethical ideals.

For example, the Milwaukee, Wisconsin, Yeshiva Elementary School included a technology policy in their Parent Handbook (September 2013), based on a belief that "internet use and abuse have led to serious family and community concerns" (p. 9). Yeshiva's technology policy recommended that the family's home computers have filters to block social networking sites and pornography, and that children's Internet usage should be monitored and that students should not have email accounts unless parents oversaw them. Students at Yeshiva Elementary did not have access to the Internet at the school.

In addition, Twin Tiers Christian Academy (2018), in Breesport, New York, framed technology use as a privilege that must be used in a "considerate, ethical, moral and legal manner." While it acknowledged the educational benefits of digital technology, the school remained wary of its "potential negative implications." Its technology use policy for students expected them to use digital technology for educational purposes only and were warned against "accessing, viewing, downloading, displaying, transmitting, creating or otherwise processing or disseminating material" that was deemed inappropriate, pornographic, obscene, lewd, vulgar or hurtful.

Influences of digital technologies

Some interviewees' cultural and ethical values framed their engagement with digital technologies, while for other interviewees religious beliefs determined their interactions with new media. Still other interviewees based their decisions about their usage of digital media on what they perceived to be the potential positive or negative effects of new technologies on their lives and identities. Several interviewees felt that it was important to set boundaries for their family's usage of digital technologies, because they believed that without human restraint, excessive new media use could take over their lives. These individuals said that they exerted control over their use of digital technology by critically evaluating each technology's strengths and weaknesses before deciding which new media to use. In addition, they said they also limited their children's screen time and monitored their own usage of digital media. About one-third of interviewees said that it would be "just fine" if all digital technology was taken away and a few said they thought the U.S. would be a better place to live if all digital media disappeared and people were encouraged to focus more on face-to-face communication.

Some interviewees said that limiting the use of social media has helped them be more productive with their leisure time. For example, Stephanie, a 33-year-old mother of two school-age children from Orlando, Florida, explained that she initially became active on social media when her children were young:

> It was a way for me to stay connected with friends when my daughters were babies and I was home all the time. But I started spending too much time on Twitter – time that I should have been spending playing with my daughters.

Stephanie said that after she realized how much time she was wasting online, she stopped Twitter "cold turkey" and found that she has had much more time now that she has controlled her social media usage.

David, a 65-year-old retired physician from Northern California, also discussed his efforts to limit his personal use of digital technologies. David rejected all social media and called Twitter and Facebook "a time suck." He considered entertainment programming on television "boring and stupid" and said that he only watched TV news. While David did not stream movies, he occasionally went out to a movie theatre to watch a film. David owned a smartphone and used it to send brief texts and make calls. A bicycle app that recorded the time and distance of each of his rides was the only app on David's smartphone and said that he liked the app because he could share his riding information with his friends. David owned an iPad, which he used to respond to email and read medical journals and *The Washington Post* and *The New York Times* each day. He also owned a laptop but said that he rarely used it because his primary interaction with digital technology was "for consuming content not creating it." David read books on his iPad when he traveled, but at home only read hardcover books. Overall, David felt that he managed his use of digital media well so that it enhanced his life and he said that technology "doesn't overwhelm my existence or take over my day so I don't feel the need to take a vacation from it."

In contrast to some interviewees distaste for many new technologies, other interviewees spoke about the positive impact that some digital technologies have had on their lives. Overall, smartphones were the most popular digital technology with the people I interviewed. Forty-one interviewees said that while they were ambivalent about some new media, they would not want to give up their smartphones. As Margaret, a 73-year-old retiree from Montana, said: "I feel so much safer driving with my phone – knowing that I can call someone if I have a problem, get directions or even pull up a map of where I'm going." Margaret said that she also used Google Maps to find nearby restaurants and gas stations.

Margaret was not the only interviewee to mention Google Maps. Twenty-seven other interviewees also considered it their favorite app and most of them admitted that they would be lost if they had to drive without it. More than two dozen interviewees ranked *The New York Times* app their favorite app because it made it much easier to read the newspaper on their phones. Twelve interviewees said online banking apps for their smartphones were their top choice of app, while many others also enjoyed having a camera on their phones. Liam, a 57-year-old businessman from Charlotte, North Carolina, said that before he had a camera on his phone:

> I'd never taken a photo – but now I'm snapping pics all the time. I've taken pictures of parts I need for repair work and shown them to the clerks at the hardware store. It's much easier than trying to bring equipment in. And when you find what you need then you just delete the pic – easy.

Other interviewees also liked apps for Skype, Snapchat, Candy Crush Saga, Instagram, What'sApp and Words With Friends.

6 Online privacy concerns

Always listening

As discussed in Chapter 2, the Internet of Things is a network of smart tools and devices physically connected to the Internet that collect and exchange data. There are currently about 8.4 billion smart devices in circulation, which include light bulbs, thermostats and plugs, security cameras, refrigerators and vacuums. Yet, about half of the smart devices now in use are smart televisions, smart speakers and other intelligent listening devices that serve as personal assistants for their owners (Ranger 2018). Voice-activated A.I. speaker devices like Google Assistant, Amazon Alexa and Apple Siri are always on and unless manually disabled, they wait for a wake-up prompt like "OK Google," "Alexa" or "Hey, Siri" in order to connect with other smart devices to access information and complete specific tasks.

Within the Internet of Things, medical devices like pacemakers and defibrillators transmit information to doctors and hospitals. Genealogy companies like Ancestry.com and 23andMe not only track their clients' and family members' history based on DNA from saliva samples, but they also share their clients' genetic information with law enforcement officials and other agencies. Search engines track individuals' browsing activity so that they can target specific ads to them, and online retailers follow people's purchasing patterns and hope to sell them more products by recommending other related goods and services (Whitney 2018). Smart devices have continuous access to people, even in their homes, and some of these devices collect and record data and conversations without a wake-up direction or their owners' explicit permission. Such concerns are prompting some technology analysts and researchers to ask: "In a world in which these personal assistants are always listening for our voices and recording our requests, have we given up on any expectation of privacy within our own homes?" (Edwards 2017a, p. 28).

Privacy issues and security threats figure prominently in the technology resistance research and constitute a main component of Morrison and Gomez's (2014) typology describing people's rationale for resisting digital technologies. Considerations about what constitutes the public and private realms as well as privacy concerns about digital media usage are also being raised by government agencies, politicians, technology experts, physicians and journalists. In addition, the vast majority of individuals I interviewed for this project raised privacy concerns regarding the ways personal information was used online; their concerns are addressed in the following two chapters. This chapter focuses on issues related to the intrusion of digital technologies into the private sphere, particularly as it relates to digital listening devices that can record people's conversations and track their movements and actions. This chapter also addresses privacy risks associated with the online disclosure of personal information and security concerns related to online banking, while Chapter 7 focuses on security and privacy concerns specifically directed toward the use of social media.

Smart devices and privacy

In 2017, Vizio, the second largest smart television maker in North America, paid $2.2 million to settle spying charges brought by the New Jersey attorney general and the Federal Trade Commission. Visio had collected viewing data on millions of its Internet-connected TVs, without the consent or the knowledge of owners, and had then sold this data to "analytics companies, media companies, and advertisers" (Maheshwari 2017). Vizio's interactive software, installed without smart television owners' knowledge, gathered data on audience members' viewing habits, targeted ads to other smart devices that the viewers used and assessed advertisements' effectiveness based on tracking "all the internet-enabled gadgets in a home" (Maheshwari 2017). Following the judgment, Vizio said it now provided a prominently placed opt in notice on all of its smart TVs and that the company currently only used data from individuals who accepted their automated content recognition (ACR) policy.

While Vizio has maintained that their ACR program currently only collected data on smart television owners who opted in, many people remain concerned about the surveillance capabilities of smart televisions, smart speakers and other digital technologies. A 2018 survey by the Pew Research Center found that most Americans had privacy concerns about how their personal information was being collected and used and they wanted more government regulation in order to secure the privacy of their personal information. Ninety-one percent of Americans in the Pew survey reported that they felt they had lost control over the way their personal information was collected and used, while 80 percent of social media users were concerned about how their information was accessed by advertisers and businesses (Rainie 2018).

The U.S. Federal Trade Commission has estimated that by 2020 there will be 50 billion Internet-connected devices in circulation, while the research company Ovum determined that in the next few years the number of smart devices using digital assistants would outnumber the number of people in the world. Digital assistants currently offer users virtual guidance, providing them with general facts and information, setting alarms, reading audio books out loud and crafting shopping lists. For example, Amazon's voice-activated personal assistant Alexa works with Echo and Echo Dot speaker devices to play music, read weather reports, provide news updates and set alarms.

Smart device owners can also buy thousands of third-party apps that extend the utility of their smart speakers. There are fitness, weather, travel and movie apps as well as apps that look up recipes, order pizza, offer popular culture quizzes and provide choose your own adventure games. The apps for Amazon's Alexa are referred to as "skills," whereas Google assistant's apps are called "actions." In addition to its skills apps, Amazon has recently launched the Alexa Hunches function, which offers suggestions to its users based on observations and commentary. For example, "if a user says good night to Alexa, the voice assistant might note that a porch light is on and offer to turn it off" (Weise 2018).

Smart device research

A recent Reuters Institute study on how people in the U.S. and the U.K. were using voice-activated smart speakers found that interviewees considered voice devices appealing because "they act differently. They provide focused information when summoned and, for the moment at least, the lack of a screen means less distraction" (Newman 2018, p. 19). However, the Reuters' study found that most interviewees were extremely frustrated with digital devices and hoped that smart speakers would ultimately help them to spend less time with screens. "Respondents felt overwhelmed, assaulted by technology and often by news as well. Many spend all day at work on screens or looking at their smartphones." Focus group members in the Reuters' study, who did not own smart speakers, reported that privacy issues were a fundamental concern that kept them from using smart devices. Many interviewees said that news reports about large technology companies listening to their private conversations made them worried about their security and they expressed concerns about technology platforms "collecting data to sell advertising or goods" (Newman 2018, p. 20).

Smart devices often provide location services that track users' current location and final destination, including their mode of transportation. However, when smartphone users accept location services in order to get weather, traffic information or local news, about 75 companies currently receive that location information and use the data for advertising and sales purposes. According to a 2018 analysis by *The New York Times*, the mobile location industry has become a new way to collect, analyze and sell people's personal data. While location businesses suggest that when smartphone users "enable location services, their data is fair game," the *Times* determined that the permissions explanations provided by location apps were misleading or incomplete: "An app may tell users that granting access to their location will help them get traffic information, but not mention that the data will be shared and sold. That disclosure is often buried in a vague privacy policy" (Valentino-DeVries, Singer, Keller and Krolik 2018).

Recently, technology journalist Kashmir Hill and investigative journalist and engineer Surya Mattu conducted a two-month smart home experiment to learn more about when and how smart devices collected data on users. Attempting to understand what information was reported back to manufacturers and how it was being used, Mattu built a special router to monitor network activity on 18 smart devices that were connected to the Internet in Hill's home. Hill and Mattu discovered that during the two-month test period, there was constant digital activity between the smart devices and its manufacturers – even when Hill and her family were out of town. While all the smart devices routinely shared data with manufacturers, the most consistent data sharing occurred with the Amazon Echo, which contacted its manufacturer's servers every three minutes, whether it was being used or not, watching, gathering data and sharing specific personal information on the Hill household. Although Hill never opted in to any ACR programs, the journalists found that during the two-month experiment all 18 smart devices were being used for data mining and to target, profile and spy on Hill's family. Overall, Hill and Mattu (2018) determined that it was easy for people to forget that, when connected to the Internet, everyday household items like coffeemakers, vacuums, televisions and lights "are spying on you."

The U.K. government privacy adviser Gilad Rosner, who founded the Internet of Things Privacy Forum, has insisted that smart digital devices have brought with them new surveillance challenges and privacy concerns. He noted that as smart devices become more mainstream, the data from these devices could impact individuals' privacy and their fundamental freedoms. Rosner has warned that data from smart devices could be combined with other information in ways that might "lead to false accusations, threats to employment or restrict a person's freedom of expression" (DaPonte 2018, p. 88).

Although providers of digital assistants like Google and Amazon have maintained that smart devices only process and record audio information after they are triggered by a voice command or by pushing a button, privacy advocates have shared a couple of recent high-profile examples of digital assistants that went rogue in an effort to warn consumers about the increasing reach of the Internet of Things. For example, in Portland, Oregon, an Amazon Echo personal assistant device recorded a conversation between a husband and wife in their home on May 2018, and after recording their conversation the device's virtual assistant Alexa sent a voice message recording of their conversation to one of the husband's employees. The couple learned about what happened when the employee called them and described their conversation. While Amazon said that Alexa had misinterpreted elements of the couple's conversation, the wife said that the Echo was close to her at the time of their conversation and the smart device had not requested permission to record or send an audio recording. In addition, in March 2018, several Amazon users reported hearing their virtual assistant Alexa laugh at them at various times without any prompts from them to do so. In response, Amazon explained that Alexa had mistakenly heard a laugh prompt and had responded by laughing. To help alleviate the problem, Amazon said it had changed the laugh prompt from "Alexa, laugh" to "Alexa, can you laugh?" (Chokshi 2018).

Researchers in the U.S. and China suggest that problems with virtual assistants, like those with Alexa, may be the result of voice recognition systems being activated by frequencies that are inaudible to the human ear. In recent studies, researchers have sent hidden commands in music and spoken text to Google's Assistant, Amazon's Alexa and Apple's Siri, secretly activating the A.I. systems on smartphones and other smart devices without their owners' knowledge and instructing them to perform certain tasks. Known as DolphinAttack by Chinese researchers, this technique can manipulate smart devices to take pictures, make phone calls, open specific websites and/or send text messages. However, researchers warn that in the wrong hands, simply by accessing music playing on the radio, "the technology could be used to unlock doors, wire money or buy stuff online" (Smith 2018).

Privacy advocates have also highlighted recent patent applications, filed by Google and Amazon, for devices designed to listen for mood shifts and emotions in the human voice. For example, Amazon's "voice sniffer algorithm" patent would analyze users' emotions on a variety of smart devices from real-time audio in order to present users with targeted ads, offers and memberships, while a Google patent application for determining speakers' moods would draw on the "volume of the user's voice, detected breathing rate, crying" and potential medical conditions in order to personalize its content. The device could even recognize a user's piece of clothing and combine it with his/her browser history in order to provide that user with movie recommendations (Maheshwari 2018).

Interviewees' privacy concerns

More than half of the people I interviewed were concerned about issues of privacy related to the use of digital technologies. Sean, a 53-year-old business owner from Seattle, expressed views echoed by many other interviewees who were in their 40s or older. As Sean explained: "I am concerned that the new smartphones can trace your movements, and that intrusion into my privacy terrifies me." He said that concerns about his family's privacy have led him and his wife to leave their smartphones on the kitchen counter at night and that his privacy worries have kept him from purchasing smart devices or a personal assistant for the family home:

> I may seem old-school but I consider my home my castle and I don't take my family's privacy for granted. We can live without a smart utility meter and we can turn off the lights by ourselves. The thought of anyone being able to watch my children playing or even sleeping, makes me ill.

Many interviewees distinguished expectations of privacy in the public realm from their assumptions of privacy in their personal lives. While most interviewees accepted surveillance activities in public areas and venues, the vast majority of people said that, like Sean, any intrusion into their private lives was inappropriate. As Patrick, a 44-year-old small business owner from Indianapolis, Indiana, explained:

> I'm OK with security cameras in grocery stores, malls and banks and I can live with them at major intersections and toll booths and even at concerts and other public places where lots of people

get together. But they have no place in my home. The idea of my smartphone or computer spying on me or tracking where I go is totally wrong and unacceptable to me.

Most interviewees did not support the use of smart home devices and referred to them as "creepy," "scary," "wasteful" and/or "frightening." Several interviewees said they never used Siri or Alexa on their smartphones because they did not see their usefulness and they would not use any smart home devices because they preferred to do certain tasks on their own. Rebecca, a 24-year-old personal assistant from Nashville, Tennessee, said she was skeptical and unsure about what information smart devices were recording and keeping: "I find smart home systems uncomfortable and unnecessary. They don't offer any easier lifestyle, just another extra step. When in reality anyone can manually do the same things that they offer, just as quickly and easily." Similarly, Susan, a 31-year-old dog groomer from Orlando, said that smart devices:

> freak me out. I know they pick up certain words but in order to do that they have to be listening all the time. I can't believe they're listening every minute of the day. I don't even have Siri on my phone let alone new devices that can glitch whenever. I like my privacy.

Interviewees in their 20s and 30s were more likely to embrace the growth of the Internet of Things, particularly in the public realm. Several people spoke of the networking of digital technologies as the wave of the future. As Danny, a 29-year-old restaurant manager in Portland, Oregon, explained:

> I can't wait until all technologies in my life and work come together. When my iPad, my laptop, my voice speaker and all my household things work as one, it'll make my life so much better and easier to manage. At that point I can see personal robots entering the mainstream and I hope by then I'll be able to afford to buy one – it'll be my own personal assistant.

Several younger interviewees referred to smart devices like Amazon Echo and Echo Dot as "cool tools," "cutting-edge," "fun to use" and "a useful speaker system." Four interviewees owned Echo Dots that they used for playing music and listening to the radio and podcasts and they said they enjoyed having them to help with their chores and to entertain their guests. One interviewee purchased an Amazon Echo for her parents as a gift, but she said that her parents would not use it because they were convinced it was "spying on them." Interviewees in their 20s and 30s were more likely to accept some potential loss of privacy connected with networked technologies; however, when it came to personal assistants interacting with smart home devices, most agreed with the concerns of older interviewees.

Even those individuals who spoke most enthusiastically about smart devices were convinced that they were listening in on their conversations. The vast majority of the people I interviewed felt that smart devices were recording private aspects of their daily lives and they were concerned with how the constant listening of the devices might be affecting their privacy. Martha, a 20-year-old student from Chicago, echoed the contradictory feelings that several other interviewees had about smart devices:

> I believe that smart home systems are becoming more of a stand-ard or regular technology in today's day and age. A part of me is a little bit terrified of them because they are always listening and invading personal privacy in a sense. However, I do think they can be very beneficial especially when it comes to setting alarms and security.

Five interviewees referenced a 2015 Arkansas murder case, in which smart devices provided investigators with crucial evidence that led them to indict the homeowner. The homeowner had invited friends to come over to his house to watch a football game and the next morning one friend was found dead in his hot tub. Data from the homeowner's iPhone showed that he had made phone calls after he told police he had gone to sleep. In addition, his Amazon Echo had recorded conversations between the homeowner and the man who died and a smart utility meter showed an excessive use of water around the time of the crime (Edwards 2017a).

While the case was dismissed in December 2017, because the evidence supported more than one explanation for the death, the five interviewees felt that investigators had crossed a line by using data from the homeowner's own smart devices. As Megan, a 38-year-old technology manager from San Francisco, California, said:

> The Arkansas murder case is insane. Nobody expects the police to come into their home and use their smartphone and house-hold property against them. I know we're living in a connected world, but I still have an expectation of privacy in my own home.

> It's crazy to think that just because someone used a lot of water in the house that night that the guy was covering up a murder – maybe one of them just took a long shower.

Other interviewees like Denver musician Roy were also concerned with the connections that investigators made using the homeowner's smart device data:

> I worry about convicting someone based on information from their personal devices. Who hasn't said they were going to bed and then texted or called someone before falling asleep? The trouble with this type of data is you don't know the whole story – the smartphone can't tell you what was going on in the house at the time – it just records what it hears. This is personal information and the police shouldn't be able to use this data against us.

Data breaches and security concerns

In 2018, data breaches once again hit record levels, a multiyear trend of governments, social media and businesses failing to keep its data safe that the Infosec Institute (2018) has determined "emphasizes how much of an impact a combination of lax security practices and the evolution of cybercrime tactics can have on privacy matters." Infosec referenced the March 2018 Equifax data breach, which exposed 143 million people's personal data, to illustrate how a single vulnerability in a Web application has impacted individuals' privacy. In addition, Infosec has determined that along with policing cybercriminals, the lack of transparency in companies' privacy terms, conditions and policies, the collection of unnecessary data, the inappropriate sharing of personal data and the inadequate disposal of personal data all currently presented major privacy threats.

On May 25, 2018, the European Union implemented the General Data Protection Regulation (GDPR), which protects the processing of personal data and provides protections for individuals in the E.U. affected by data breaches. In 2017, the E.U. had fined Google $2.7 billion because the company had manipulated online shopping markets. Since its implementation, the GDPR now required Google and other technology companies to obtain users' consent before the companies could use their data (Brooker 2018). However, in January 2019, French regulators fined Google almost $57 million for violating the GDPR because it did not fully disclose to users how they collected their personal information. In addition, Google did not properly obtain users' consent for ads that they showed to them (Romm 2019).

Although data breaches and cyberattacks have continued to increase and in the first nine months of 2018, approximately 3,700 data breaches occurred; at this point, the U.S. does not have any protections for its citizens. According to Grothaus (2018), the largest data scandal of 2018 was Cambridge Analytica's harvesting of at least 87 million Facebook users' data without their knowledge. Cambridge Analytica subsequently sold the data it had harvested to Donald Trump's campaign, who used the information to target Facebook users during the presidential election campaign of 2016. The Cambridge Analytica Facebook data scandal and other Facebook data breaches are addressed more fully in Chapter 7.

The scope of recent data breaches has been enormous. For example, the Florida market firm Exactis exposed the records of 340 million businesses and people on a publicly accessible server. In June 2018, it was discovered that peoples' names, email addresses and personal information, including individuals' religion, smoking status, hobbies and number of children, if any, had been made public. While on November 30, 2018, Marriott announced that hackers had accessed personal information regarding one half of a billion of its hotel guests. The hackers had accessed names, home addresses, phone numbers, email addresses, passport numbers, birth dates, payment card numbers and expiration dates and other information on 327 million guests and had also accessed names, addresses, email addresses and other information on 173 million additional guests (Grothaus 2018).

According to data security experts, employment-related data breaches have also increased. Employees' social security numbers, bank accounts, biometric data and other personal information has been accessed on lost or stolen laptops and from phishing scams, through which employees have received emails from a cybercriminal, impersonating a senior executive or a vendor, asking for log-in information or requesting employees' W-2s. Employees' personal information has also been accessed by external hackers, third-party providers like payroll vendors and even by disgruntled employees (McGregor 2018).

Several technology-savvy interviewees, from a variety of backgrounds, ages and regions of the country, discussed their concerns with sharing personal information online. Randall, a 58-year-old East Coast professor of business, used a variety of online websites for his research and classroom management, but said that because of the data breaches he has seen and heard about he was cautious about sharing his personal data online:

> Over the years, I've received quite a few seemingly authentic requests for private information via email. Several of them were

supposedly requests from my university human resources department. But in each case the email asked for my bank account routing number or my social security number and that made me uncomfortable so I began to routinely check each email request for private information with my university's technology help desk.

Randall said after learning that several emails were actually phishing scams, he has gotten in the habit of checking all email requests before sharing any private information online: "These days I always check and even when it's an authentic request, I prefer not to share my information online."

Similarly, Megan, a 38-year-old technology manager from San Francisco, California, addressed the risks associated with disclosing personal information online:

> I have learned a lot about techniques and technologies that are available for getting information off of the Internet. This is something that we talk about a lot. I have learned about different capabilities and about the type of access that some people in our lab have.

Megan said that many of the people she works with also have concerns about online information: "I think just realizing that these people who know a tremendous amount about what's possible and seeing them so skeptical and concerned that I realized online privacy is something I should be more aware of."

Popular culture and security concerns

As they did with issues connected to A.I., several interviewees referenced popular culture to help them explain their feelings about privacy and security issues related to digital technologies. Interviewees mentioned the realistic depictions of electronic surveillance, hacking and social engineering on the TV shows *The Wire* and *Mr. Robot*, and they thought *The Americans* helped them to understand how spies bypassed security measures in order to access important private information. Multiple people referred to police procedurals like *NCIS*, *Law and Order* and *The Wire*, where the investigative procedure is emphasized, and said that these shows demonstrated how commonplace government and police surveillance had become. Two interviewees discussed issues of electronic surveillance in *Black Mirror*, referencing one particular episode "The Entire History of You," in which a device is implanted in people that tracks and records everything they hear and see. Both people said they found the episode "unnerving," and "frightening," particularly because it seemed "quite plausible." As Jerry, a 32-year-old electrician from Billings, Montana, explained:

> *Black Mirror* is definitely realistic and all of its episodes focus on types of surveillance. But "The Entire History of You" – that show was too intense – it left me very uneasy and wondering how soon the police will start lobbying to use tracking devices like it to help stop crime.

Interviewees also mentioned government and business surveillance in movies like *Enemy of the State* and *Snowden*. Five people brought up the films *Minority Report* and *Gattaca*, particularly as it related to the dangers of personal genetic information being hacked and getting into the wrong hands. In *Minority Report*, people are surveilled and arrested based on predictions that they may commit future crimes and in *Gattaca*, a class system developed based on individuals' genetic makeup. During her interview, Marie, a 53-year-old accountant from St. Paul, Minnesota, said:

> The main character Vincent in *Gattaca* was discriminated against because he had some genetic health concerns. In the film most babies were genetically engineered but Vincent was conceived naturally. And because he wasn't perfect – DNA wise – the only type of jobs open to him were in maintenance. I thought it was awful that he was rejected from most careers because of his DNA and every time I hear about data breaches, I wonder if sometime soon my private information will get hacked and sold.

In *Gattaca*, Vincent wanted to become an astronaut but because of his genetic makeup he was not considered physically capable of such a career. Vincent decided to buy another man's DNA which gave him access to the space program. Marie, who has diabetes, said that she understood Vincent's desire to get past his DNA and she wondered what might happen if insurance companies were able to access people's private medical information. As Marie explained:

> So I worry if insurance companies will soon be able to get private health information on people like me who have medical problems but aren't currently insured with them. If so, we might not be able to get new health insurance or if we do we'll be charged a lot more than people without any health issues.

Online banking concerns

A variety of interviewees expressed their concerns regarding the safety of their online information, specifically as it related to online banking. While banks and credit unions have instituted a number of policies to keep the accounts of its online customers secure, including the use of firewalls and antivirus protection, fraud monitoring and website encryption (Burnette 2018), 27 interviewees said they did not use online banking specifically because they had safety concerns. The majority of these interviewees described themselves as very knowledgeable about technology and banking security issues and said that they did not feel comfortable with the degree of protection afforded to bank accounts in cyberspace. Michelle, a 45-year-old accountant from Texas, said she felt that in our digital society it was important to choose a large financial institution with a top reputation:

> I've seen people get hacked after using public Wi-Fi for their online banking or having problems with a small online bank that doesn't have great security. Most of my banking is done in person but when I need to use online banking, I use my home private network and I regularly change my password.

John, a 30-year-old technology analyst working in Washington D.C., was particularly concerned about using a smartphone for any banking transactions and he felt that the majority of online bank users did not take the risks seriously:

> Most people take it for granted that when they access their bank accounts on their smartphones that the information is safe and protected. This is my area and let me tell you, that's crazy. I don't trust mobile banking and I don't recommend using mobile banking. It's not all that safe. There are too many ways that your information can be compromised. If you have to bank online, use your computer to access your accounts. Trust me, you'll be better off in the long run.

John said that in his work he has seen a variety of phishing scams that have defrauded unsuspecting individuals:

> One fraudster sent out emails pretending to represent a well-known bank and asking its customers to update their account

information. The email was very professional and the bank logo was even reproduced on the email. It is my understanding that quite a few people were defrauded by the scam.

Sean said he was also concerned about online banking and explained that after reading several news articles about businesses getting hacked, he also began to worry about the vulnerability of his company's online records. "I woke up a few times in a cold sweat, worrying that my business and personal accounts might get hacked and so I started looking into security options." After doing his research, Sean said he "sleeps better now" because he had contracted with a privacy security firm that monitors his personal and business bank accounts as well as his credit cards and major purchases.

In addition to the technology-savvy individuals who worried about the security of online banking, eight older interviewees said that they felt more comfortable with the security of brick and mortar banks and felt that the relationships they had developed with their local banks would help to keep their accounts safer. Edith, a 66-year-old retiree from Chicago, Illinois, explained this perspective:

> I've been going to the same bank for more than 30 years – I know the bank manager on a first name basis and most of the tellers know me. I feel more secure about my money when I make my deposits directly at the bank.

Edith said that she received great customer service at her bank:

> They always check my balance and a few times over the years they have noticed what they thought were questionable activities on my account and they've have called me to check them out. Why would I want to give that up for an app?

Interestingly, 41 interviewees of varying ages and locations had no problem using online banking either on their smartphones, computers or tablets. For example, Mike, the 31-year-old writer from Brooklyn, New York, who used a typewriter for his creative writing, spoke enthusiastically about the ease of banking online:

> I travel frequently for work and mobile banking makes my hectic life much easier. I have an app for my bank on my iPhone that allows me to manage my accounts, make deposits, pay bills, transfer money

and set travel alerts quickly and easily. My banking information is encrypted so I don't worry about getting hacked. I'm not a huge fan of digital technology but I enjoy the ease of online banking.

Similarly, Vicky, a 64-year-old vinyl fan from Toledo, Ohio, considered her banking app one of the best parts of having a smartphone.

> I love, love, love to bank on my smartphone. I'm still amazed that all I need to do to deposit a check is take a picture of it with my phone and it's deposited in my account. That's pretty cool. I also like paying bills online and not having to write checks anymore. It makes banking much more user friendly. I remember having to go to the bank to deposit my paycheck each Friday. It always took so long that I usually missed my lunch because I had to get back to work. Now I can do my banking anyplace and anytime.

Time to push back?

Drawing on insights from Foucault, media and communication theorists have suggested that the widespread use of the Internet has led to the creation of a "digital panopticon," in which all actions become observed and analyzed through computer surveillance. As this happens, businesses and governments gather an excessive amount of data about customers and citizens, which often results in greater influence and "more effective political and marketing control" (Sparks 2013, p. 32).

Philip Zimmermann, Internet Hall of Fame inductee and founder of the mobile encryption company Silent Circle, has warned the public about the mass surveillance of law-abiding citizens. Insisting that excessive surveillance was contrary to democratic ideals, he has repeatedly maintained that people needed to "push back" against what he has called "the golden age of surveillance." For Zimmermann, traffic cameras and facial recognition software used by western governments have resulted in arrests and prosecutions that have challenged citizens' long-held beliefs about privacy protections. "We have to roll this back. People who are not suspected of committing crimes should not have information collected and stored in a database" (quoted in Garside 2015). Zimmermann has said that individuals' privacy has also been weakened by the huge stockpiles of personal data collected by companies like Facebook and Google, often without the knowledge or consent of users, which has encouraged other companies and governments to attempt to get this information.

In response to concerns like Zimmermann's and responding to major privacy breaches, political manipulation, prejudice, abuse, discrimination, hate and other online threats, Tim Berners-Lee, the creator of the World Wide Web, has called for a "Contract for the Web" that would focus on protecting people's Internet freedoms and rights. Envisioning the contract will serve "humanity, science, knowledge and democracy," Berners-Lee has committed to keeping the Internet accessible and affordable, "respecting consumer privacy and personal data," so that they can use the Internet safely and without fear, and developing new technologies to make sure that the Web becomes "a public good that puts people first" (quoted in Sample 2018).

Berners-Lee explained that he initially released the source code for the Web for free, a decision that was intended to insure the Web would become "a radical tool for democracy," open and accessible for all. While he felt from the beginning that the Web could transform businesses, governments and societies, he also understood that in the wrong hands his invention could "become a destroyer of worlds" (quoted in Brooker 2018). "Devastated" about recent Web abuses, Berners-Lee is now determined to use his coding skills and celebrity status to "reclaim the Web from corporations and return it to its democratic roots." Foreseeing the re-decentralization of the Web, Berners-Lee is currently working with a small group of developers, on Solid, a platform that would "give individuals, rather than corporations, control of their own data" (quoted in Brooker 2018). Ultimately, Berners-Lee remained hopeful that other coders and ordinary people would rise up against the "anti-human" platforms created from the increasing corporate control of digital technologies and take back control of the Web.

7 The case of social media

Many of the concerns regarding social media have focused on issues associated with data mining, manipulating public opinion and expectations of privacy. Researchers have warned about social media platforms using personal data to shape individuals' behavior. Politicians, former technology executives and physicians have raised concerns regarding social media's role in creating and reinforcing isolation and addictive behaviors as well as providing a platform for hate, propaganda, mistruths, fake news and lies.

The notion of opting in or opting out of digital media in order to develop a person's identity or to assert an individual's independence, authority and dominance over new technologies is a theme addressed throughout this book that is particularly relevant to individuals' reactions to social media. Decisions about how to engage with social media are a core way many interviewees asserted agency over digital media and their views on social media that have factored into the crafting of their personal identities. Some interviewees said they have never used social media, while others were former Facebook or Twitter users who recently chose to opt out of all social media because of their growing concerns regarding issues of privacy and security. Other interviewees have taken breaks from social media at particular times for specific reasons, while still others picked one or two platforms that they used and chose not to engage with the rest of social media. While there are a variety of social media platforms available to the public, Facebook is currently the largest, and its development and recent public challenges provide a lens through which to begin a consideration of people's reactions to social media.

Specifically, this chapter addresses privacy and security issues in social media and considers the many reasons why people choose to use or not use social media. Beginning with the development of Facebook, this chapter draws on interviewees' commentary to reinforce an understanding of the role of human agency in peoples' choices about how they interact with digital technologies. This chapter also considers interviewees' opinions of Facebook and other social media, and in addition it addresses how some interviewees' construct their personal identities through the decisions they make regarding social media.

The development of Facebook

While data mining, security and privacy issues and the manipulating of public opinion have been raised about all social media, in recent years much of the criticism and commentary has focused specifically on Facebook. The Facebook social media site was launched on February 4, 2004, and was initially open only to students at Harvard University. It slowly began expanding on college campuses, dropped "the" from its name and by September 2006, Facebook became available to every person with an email address who was at least 13 years of age. Facebook users totaled 12 million in December 2006 and by September 2009 there were 300 million Facebook users (Boyd 2018). In 2018, more than 2.2 billion people logged onto Facebook at least once each month. Facebook currently mines the data of all its users, collecting huge amounts of information and providing advertisers with the tools to target users with micro-precision. Critics charge that without involving any human judgment or intervention, Facebook's algorithm, "and its endless capacity to aggregate people's predilections and assign them a dollar value," has turned its users into products (Bauerlein and Jeffery 2018). Facebook's business model currently generates more advertising revenue each year than the combined revenue for all American newspapers. Chairman and C.E.O. of Facebook, Mark Zuckerberg, currently owns about 60 percent of Facebook's stock. Facebook along with Apple, Google and Amazon are currently the four largest companies dominating the Internet (Osnos 2018).

Recently, many of the concerns about Facebook have focused on privacy, data mining and manipulating public opinion through propaganda and disinformation campaigns. Researchers have warned about using personal data to shape individuals' behavior. For example, in 2014, it was discovered that Facebook had experimented on approximately 700,000 Facebook users, manipulating their news feeds by removing all negative or positive posts in order to determine if they could influence users' emotions. The experiment was successful; users' feelings were affected by their news feeds and Facebook discovered "it could cause massive-scale contagion via social networks" (Bilton

2014a). Technology leaders have also raised concerns regarding what they saw as Facebook's "role in exacerbating isolation, outrage, and addictive behaviors" (Osnos 2018). As Facebook has expanded globally, critics have increasingly charged that the social media platform has inflamed political tensions by spreading hate speech, misinformation and lies. Critics have showcased the huge increase in Facebook users in countries like Myanmar (Burma), explaining that because Facebook had been preinstalled on cell phones and could be accessed for free in these countries it had become synonymous with the Internet. (Oliver 2018).

Technology researchers discovered Facebook's power to influence individuals' voting behavior during the 2010 U.S. midterm election, when they found that showing users pictures of their friends who had already voted and offering them the option of accessing an "I Voted" button dramatically increased voter participation. "It became a running joke among employees that Facebook could tilt an election just by choosing where to deploy its 'I Voted' button" (Osnos 2018). However, it was not until the 2016 U.S. presidential election that many of the problems associated with Facebook began to be made public. During the election campaign, some political partisans profited by infiltrating Facebook's automated system in order to spread large amounts of misinformation, fake news and "toxic political clickbait" to susceptible Facebook users. In addition, Russian agents targeted approximately 150 million Americans on Facebook, Twitter and Instagram in an effort to spread propaganda and lies and to "sow political chaos and help Trump win" (Osnos 2018).

Just a few months later, the U.S. and British press reported that the personal information of 87 million Facebook users had been accessed by a researcher and sold to Cambridge Analytica, a political consulting firm hired by Trump and other Republicans. Cambridge Analytica touted its ability to manipulate voters' behavior through the use of psychological marketing techniques like drawing on people's fears and anxieties or exacerbating their anger and hatred. Perhaps, most disheartening was the disclosure that Facebook had known since December 2015 that because of a data breach, Cambridge Analytica and other businesses had gained access to millions of users' private information. However, Facebook kept the information secret and only acknowledged the problem after it was discovered, more than a year later, by reporters at *The Guardian* and *The New York Times* (Bauerlein and Jeffery 2018).

Facebook's facial recognition tool has recently been showcased by the company as a digital technology able to catch criminals and as a way to protect individuals' identity. However, some privacy groups, consumer organizations, civil liberties experts and politicians maintain that Facebook's facial recognition software violates an individual's privacy because it does not obtain the proper consent of its users and could ultimately be used to create a "mass surveillance system." Facebook's facial recognition tool scans the faces of unidentified people in videos or photographs, and then matches their facial patterns and codes to databases of previously identified people. Facebook has insisted that its users control facial recognition through their facial recognition setting. However, an attorney with the digital rights group the Electronic Frontier Foundation said that Facebook scans every photo, even when users' facial recognition settings are turned off. Other critics have suggested that by promoting their facial recognition software as an identity protection tool, Facebook has been attempting to manipulate users' consent to turn on facial recognition (Singer 2018).

The delete Facebook movement

After years of giving Facebook the benefit of the doubt, the Cambridge Analytica scandal and other privacy concerns have impacted Facebook's reputation and its bottom line. Citizens are increasingly worried about the collection and the use of their private information (Maheshwari 2018). A coalition of progressive groups are concerned about Facebook's size, reach and access to people's personal information and has asked the Federal Trade Commission to divide the company into smaller units. Facebook's stock price has dropped significantly, its user base is stagnant and it is currently under investigation in the U.S. and Europe by the Department of Justice, the Federal Trade Commission, the F.B.I. and the Securities and Exchange Commission. Facebook is also being investigated by the British Parliament, the European Union and by senior officials in other countries, including Canada, Belgium and Argentina.

Throughout the years, Facebook has granted access to its social network to other companies, including Microsoft, Amazon, Yahoo, Spotify and Netflix. "Every corporate partner that integrated Facebook data into its online products helped drive the platform's expansion, bringing in new users, spurring them to spend more time on Facebook and driving up advertising revenue" (Dance, LaForgia and Confessore 2018). In exchange, Facebook has received important information back from its corporate partners. In December 2018, a British parliamentary committee investigating online misinformation released confidential Facebook documents and emails previously "under seal" in the U.S., which showed "how Facebook executives treated data as the company's most valuable resource and often wielded it to gain a strategic advantage" (Satariano and Isaac 2018). In an attempt to undermine competitors, Facebook provided special access to users' data for some advertisers like Netflix, Lyft and Airbnb, while it excluded access to data for other rival companies.

In addition to concerns about privacy and security issues, Facebook's data mining practices and the Cambridge Analytica scandal have also led to a delete movement by technology executives, celebrities and online groups. In March 2018, Elon Musk, chief executive of Tesla and SpaceX, took to Twitter to announce his decision to #DeleteFacebook. Musk deleted Facebook pages for both Tesla and Space X, but kept his Instagram account and his 6.9 million followers. Musk joined other technology leaders like Brian Acton (cofounder of WhatsApp) and Steve Wozniak, (cofounder of Apple), who deactivated their accounts because they were concerned about Facebook making money from individuals' personal data. Hollywood celebrities like Cher, Jim Carey, Will Ferrell and Susan Sarandon have deleted their personal Facebook pages, joining an online movement that in the wake of the Cambridge Analytica scandal has called for people to abandon the social network (Bowles 2018c).

Philosophers, religious leaders and politicians have also urged people to opt out of Facebook. For example, the November 24, 2018, Sunday Review section of *The New York Times* featured an essay by the philosopher S. Matthew Liao explaining that it was the public's moral duty to leave Facebook. Facebook's addictive and time-consuming nature, in addition to its proclivity to enhance an individual's anxiety and depression, were cited by Liao as reasons someone might have a personal duty to quit Facebook. However, most of Liao's commentary emphasized one's duty to others as the primary reason to reject Facebook. He maintained that Facebook has undermined important democratic values; he referenced Facebook spreading "white supremacist propaganda and anti-Semitic messages" in the U.S. and abroad, the Cambridge Analytica scandal, Facebook's data mining and its experiments in user manipulation to support his view that citizens have a moral obligation to leave Facebook. In addition, Liao suggested that it was a mistake to share, react, criticize or comment on an inappropriate Facebook post because "one is amplifying the message of that post and signaling that the post warrants further attention" (Liao 2018).

Facebook nonusers

There are currently millions of people worldwide who do not engage with social media, and some reasons that people reject it are addressed later in this chapter. However, there is a growing number of people who use social media but have specifically rejected Facebook. Some individuals were former MySpace users and have resisted joining the competition and some tried Facebook and quit for a variety of reasons, while others have never been on Facebook but use Twitter, Instagram or other social media platforms.

Several interviewees discussed their reasons for not engaging with Facebook. A few younger people, who were all former Facebook users, said during their interviews that they have recently opted out of Facebook. As Sam, a 20-year-old student from St. Louis, said:

> In the last year I have actually completely cut off Facebook. It feels great because I don't think any of it is really good for us at all. I've found Facebook so addictive that it's usually the case that it separates people instead of bringing them together. I know that I'm better off without it.

Justin, a 26-year-old graduate student from Detroit, Michigan, said that he has deleted his Facebook account because he found that his time on the platform was negatively affecting his friendships. As Justin explained:

> I'd spend my time looking at my news feed, liking my friends' pictures and status updates, making brief comments, but I wasn't really spending any real time with them. I wasn't hanging with my friends, connecting with them, talking to them and they began to seem distant. I feel closer to my friends now that I'm off of Facebook.

Justin said that he has maintained his Twitter account so that he can keep up with the news and contact his friends when necessary.

Some interviewees in their 40s and older, who had previously been Facebook users, said they had deleted their accounts specifically because of the Cambridge Analytica scandal. Michelle, a 45-year-old accountant from Houston, Texas, said she previously enjoyed being on Facebook and understood that her privacy would be "somewhat affected" because some of her information would be available online. However, she recently decided that the mining of millions of Americans'

data for political purposes went too far. Michelle's rationale for delet-
ing Facebook resonated with other people who I interviewed:

> I really liked keeping up with friends and family on Facebook,
> seeing pictures of their children and pets and reading about their
> vacations. But the whole Cambridge Analytica mess is too much
> for me. I can't stand that millions of people's Facebook data was
> used and people were manipulated to help Trump's campaign.
> Who does something like that? Clearly, they have no morals and
> I don't want to be affiliated in any way with Facebook anymore.

Liam, a 57-year-old businessman from North Carolina, said that while
he had debated opting out of Facebook for years and has taken breaks
from social media in the past, that the revelations about Cambridge
Analytica provided him with the needed impetus to quit Facebook
for good:

> I've had a love-hate relationship with Facebook for several years.
> I've liked keeping up with my friends, but in the last few years I've
> become tired of the toxic crap and propaganda that is so often
> presented as news. I started wondering how healthy it was for
> me to spend my time scrolling through this shit every day. And
> then I heard the news about how Cambridge Analytica illegally
> mined data from millions of Facebook users in order to manipu-
> late people about the election. That's just wrong. I've deleted my
> account and I feel real good about it. I'm relieved to be done with
> Facebook – it's one less thing to worry about.

Although many interviewees expressed their concerns regarding the
safety of their personal information on Facebook and other social media, a few older interviewees said that while they had privacy concerns
about the platform, they enjoyed using Facebook too much to give it
up. For example, while Vicki, a grandmother from Toledo, was concerned about data breaches, during her interview she explained:

> I worry about my personal information getting in the wrong hands
> but I love visiting with my old friends on Facebook, reminiscing
> with them about things we did in high school or college and re-
> living great times. So many of my friends have kept pictures of
> school activities, parties and vacations and have uploaded them
> to Facebook. It's a trip seeing all of us when we were young and at
> this point I think the good outweighs the bad.

Vicki said that she also keeps up with a small community of vinyl devotees on Facebook: "We like to share info on new releases, and out of the way places to go for albums."

Similarly, Tyler, a 67-year-old retiree from Portland, Oregon, also enjoyed connecting with old friends and family members on Facebook: "I like getting all kinds of birthday messages from all over – it's nice to know they're thinking of me." In addition, Tyler, who collects and renovates classic cars, said that he regularly connects with car enthusiasts on Facebook:

> Several of my Facebook friends are collectors and it's great to talk cars with them. Sometimes I get a lead on a great find from a Facebook friend. We also share tips on ways to find parts for older cars. At this point I don't want to quit Facebook, but that might change if they keep having security problems.

Digital natives' social media concerns

In light of high-profile data breaches and the call to delete Facebook, the public has become more concerned about the collection and use of their personal information on all social media (Maheshwari 2018). A 2018 survey found that more than two-thirds of social media users were worried about the security of their private information and felt that they had lost control of their private data (Rainie 2018). In addition, a recent survey by the news website Quartz found that almost 80 percent of its readers did not trust Facebook with their personal information. Survey respondents ranked Facebook least trustworthy among U.S. consumer technology companies. Fifty-eight percent of those surveyed were U.S.-based business people while 42 percent of respondents were business executives from other countries (Edwards 2017b).

Although unplugging from social media may be challenging for many Americans, in 2018 the Pew Research Center found that the majority of Facebook users surveyed had been taking steps to manage their social media use. Many users have changed their privacy settings and restricted access to their profiles or tried to be anonymous, while more than half of social media users have taken breaks away from Facebook when they were busy or they felt the content was too conflict ridden, political or gossipy (Rainie 2018). In addition, the vast majority of millennials (individuals born between 1981 and 1996) who were surveyed by the American Psychological Association (2017) reported that while they were comfortable with digital technologies, they also had the highest levels of stress connected with new technologies. Millennials also said that they were worried about the "negative effects of social media on their physical and mental health."

Recent studies of digital natives between the ages of 18–24, in the U.S. and the U.K. have challenged the assumption that young people are "hopelessly devoted" to Facebook, Instagram, Twitter and other social media. Researchers have found that during the last two years, digital natives have significantly changed their feelings about social media. In one U.S. survey, more than half of the respondents said that they had quit social media or were thinking about quitting at least one social media platform, while a 2018 Pew study of teenagers found that the majority were worried about spending too much time online, with 57 percent of surveyed teens indicating that they were limiting their social media use (Jiang 2018). In addition, a recent study of British teenagers found that 63 percent of them "would be happy if social media had never been invented" (Kale 2018). Teenagers have reported becoming overwhelmed by social media, and many indicated that they would like to focus on building authentic off-line friendships. Fifty-eight percent of U.S. teenagers surveyed said that they had taken at least one break from social media when they were busy with school or work or when they were "tired of the conflict or drama they could see unfolding among their peer group online" (Kale 2018).

During my interviews, the majority of men and women in their 20s and 30s spoke at length about social media. Several undergraduate and graduate students said they took breaks from social media when they were home with their families or when they felt stressed out or particularly busy with school, "preparing for an exam," "studying for finals," "working on a class project" or "writing a paper." For example, Lynn, a 21-year-old student from Milwaukee, said:

> I have taken lots of breaks from social media. If I'm very busy or stressed, I'll delete Instagram or Twitter because I find them most distracting. Without them it makes focusing much easier and relieves the stress of looking at others.

Melissa, a 25-year old graduate student from Phoenix, said that she also took social media breaks during school:

> all the time. Sometimes I get too invested in it and it distracts me from my classes so I have to take a step back. I normally delete my Facebook, Twitter and Instagram apps and live outside the

bubble. I'll ignore my Snapchats because it gets to be so much sometimes and I need to focus on my classes. We often lose the big picture with all these apps at our fingertips.

Other students discussed taking a break from social media for physical or mental health reasons. Some interviewees said they found social media "upsetting," "overwhelming" or "depressing," and they suggested that their self-esteem was affected when they compared their lives to others on Facebook, Twitter or Instagram. As Martha, a 20-year-old student from Chicago, explained:

I usually voluntarily take a break from social media when I want to focus on my mental health. I like to avoid it at times because I often compare my life to others even though I know social media is contrived and not a reflection of real life and it's unhealthy for me to do so. But seeing others' posts still impacts my self-esteem – negatively – even when I know that the posts aren't always real.

Similarly, Benji, a 29-year-old graduate student from Atlanta, also found social media depressing:

When I see Facebook posts of friends and family, traveling to exotic places, eating at wonderful restaurants, having exciting adventures, I often get depressed and sad. I think about my life as a graduate student, living in a crappy apartment, eating ramen most days and not doing much outside of school. It sucks for me to compare my life to what I see on Facebook and Instagram, so I often take social media breaks during the semester to focus on my work and feel better about myself.

Student interviewees who took a break from social media for mental health reasons reinforced the findings from a December 2018 study of undergraduates' use of Facebook, Instagram and Snapchat, published in the *Journal of Social and Clinical Psychology*. The experimental study determined that when students limited their social media usage each day to ten minutes for each platform, there was a dramatic positive effect on their well-being. Students reported being less depressed and lonely and much happier when they limited their total social media use to a maximum of 30 minutes a day (Davis 2018).

Recent research also indicates that U.S. parents have become increasingly concerned about the influence of social media and other digital technologies on their children. A 2018 Pew study found that about two-thirds of parents surveyed reported concerns about the influence of social media on their teens, and in response they were setting time restrictions for them. Seventy-one percent of parents of teens aged 13–14 said they limited their adolescents' social media access and screen time and 47 percent of parents of teens aged 15–17 reported restricting their access (Jiang 2018).

Ed, a lawyer from Atlanta, who took his family on a technology-free family vacation to Disney World, said during his interview that at this point he and his wife have successfully restricted their children's access to social media:

> We're very concerned about the effects of social media on the kids. There are too many troubling things on Facebook and we don't want them to get caught up with all the gossip and nastiness on Twitter and other social media sites. And besides I don't think it's good for their self-esteem. They already spend too much time on their screens, playing games, texting their friends and watching videos. Our oldest is only 11 and luckily we've been successful keeping the kids off of social media so far but some of their friends are already on Facebook.

Similarly, Mikayla, a 42-year-old physician from Dallas, Texas, said that she has also kept her 11-year-old son and 14-year-old daughter off social media: "With all of the mental health issues coming out about social media, I'm wary about exposing my children to it too soon. They have enough to worry about without dealing with Twitter trolls or Facebook gossip." During her interview, Mikayla said that a colleague's daughter had been bullied on social media and that it was a difficult experience for the entire family:

> My concerns about social media are not limited to the research studies that I've read. One of my associates and his family have been dealing with a very distressing situation. His daughter has been threatened and tormented on Facebook by girls in her middle school and now she is embarrassed and doesn't want to go to school anymore. She's currently being home-schooled and is in therapy but all she wants to do is stay at home. She doesn't want to go out with her friends at all anymore. Apparently, there isn't much that they can do about it and when my colleague spoke with one of the girl's parents, he was told that "all kids are doing it." It's bad enough when teenagers do mean things in person, but when

it's on social media the effect seems greater and it seems to last forever. I'll do everything I can to make sure that my children don't have to deal with cyberbullying.

Balancing social media usage

In the last few years, several prominent journalists have written about their experiences with social media and the reasons why they have decided to try and balance their social media usage. *The New York Times* columnist and reporter Nick Bilton (2014a) wrote that while his early experiences on social media "were exiting and novel," he increasingly felt that he was wasting his time. Bilton explained that "Like a virus slowly invading its victim, social media has methodically started to consume every hour of my day." In an effort to reclaim some of his time, Bilton decided to balance his social media usage by spending some time each morning reading a book. Pulitzer Prize-winning journalist Maggie Haberman (2018), who is a White House correspondent for *The New York Times*, quit Twitter in July 2018 because she felt it had become a huge drain on her time and energy. While Haberman considered Twitter a useful platform and she planned to come back to it in the future, she was concerned that in the current political climate, Twitter had become a place where:

> The viciousness, toxic partisan anger, intellectual dishonesty, motive-questioning and sexism are at all-time highs, with no end in sight. It is a place where people who are understandably upset about any number of things go to feed their anger, where the underbelly of free speech is at its most bilious.

Several interviewees discussed balancing their social media usage as an important way they asserted their dominance over digital technology. In some cases, interviewees said that balance was achieved by using only one social media platform or by restricting the total time they spent on social media. Other interviewees said they took frequent breaks from social media in order to balance their reliance on digital technologies. As Vaughn, a 38-year-old small business owner from New Mexico, reported:

> I only use Twitter, I just think Twitter's kind of perfect and it's the one platform that connects to my personal interests. By choosing only Twitter, I don't spend all my time on social media which helps me to stay in control of my media use and balance my time better.

Similarly, Karen, a 48-year-old accountant and amateur photographer from Ventura, said that she has limited her social media use to Instagram: "I use Instagram because I like taking pictures and seeing my friends' pictures. It's much easier for me to balance my technology use because I'm not on Facebook or Twitter." In contrast, Jan, a 45-year-old homemaker, said that she balanced her technology use by taking frequent breaks from it. Jan has Instagram, Facebook and Twitter accounts and said she enjoyed being on social media:

> I love keeping up with my friends on social media and sharing fun family activities. And some days I spend several hours on social media – sometimes when the kids are at school and I'm all caught up I might be on Twitter and Facebook all afternoon. But when I'm busy I take a break from it – it doesn't rule my life – I'm in charge – I just find it a fun way to pass the time. I also love to read and some days I spend my free time reading and don't go on social media at all.

Social media nonusers

The choice to never engage with social media was another way some interviewees asserted their agency over digital media. While some researchers have suggested that people who do not engage with social media are committing virtual identity suicide, approximately one-third of the people I interviewed totally rejected social media for a wide variety of reasons.

Several interviewees opted out of social media for religious, political or cultural reasons or because it did not align with their moral values. Those interviewees who practiced voluntary simplicity or were part of a back-to-the-land cultural movement, felt that social media did not promote communication or community and that it went against their goal of "protecting nature" and limiting conspicuous consumption. Interviewees who limited their digital technology use for religious reasons did not engage with social media. As Sarah, an Orthodox Jew from New York, explained:

> Social media is a distraction from the important things in this world. It's about gossip, and consumption and it encourages people to focus on silly, superficial things and to envy material things that are unnecessary. From what I've read, I think social media is unhealthy, especially for children – it's the opposite of real communication and I wouldn't want any of my children to get influenced by its focus on consumption.

Other interviewees said they rejected social media because they considered it a waste of their time and suggested that they preferred to focus on sports, hobbies, family or community activities.

Privacy concerns have also kept some interviewees from using any social media. Marie, the 53-year-old accountant from St. Paul, who worried about her private health information being hacked and sold, also expressed her concerns regarding users' privacy on social media:

> I've always been worried about the security of my information on social media sites and I don't want to have my private information so easily accessible. So that's the main reason I don't use social media. But recently, I've become more fearful about the easy access that all kinds of people have to hateful propaganda and misinformation. From what I've heard, so much content on Facebook is either trivial feel-good stories and animal pictures or its unfiltered, unedited hate-filled garbage, lies and fake news. And it seems like a bad idea for it to be so readily available to all types of people because I think it might encourage some people to do horrible things.

Business professor Randall said that his concerns about data breaches have also kept him from engaging with social media and that his lack of social media use has become a part of his identity: "I've never trusted Facebook or Twitter to keep my personal information safe which is why I've made the decision to stay away from all social media." Randall said that he has become known around campus as being against social media, a label that he was comfortable embracing:

> My students sometimes call me their anti-social media professor – so now that's part of my university identity. But apart from my security concerns, I'm glad that I don't have to interact with my students on Facebook or Twitter. I'd probably be annoyed with them if I saw they were posting on Facebook or tweeting updates when they should be studying for my exam.

Although researchers like Bobkowski and Smith (2013) have suggested that "non-adopters" of social media had fewer friends, were less socially active and even had "few meaningful friendships" (p. 777), some interviewees said that not being on social media has helped them develop more meaningful relationships. For example, Andrea, a designer at a Boston technology company, who is in her 30s, chose not to engage with any social media because she felt that Facebook and Twitter encouraged people to settle for superficial relationships. As Andrea explained:

> I started to see that for a lot of my peers there were certain types of relationships that they would only maintain through Facebook. So, there were all of these acquaintances that they would be connected to, they would be friends with on Facebook and maybe they would never have any interaction with those people in person or even on electronic media in any way. It seemed to me to be more about the idea of maintaining a connection with these people as opposed to really getting anything meaningful or giving anything meaningful to the relationship.

Andrea was first exposed to a precursor of Facebook called "Plans" when she was an undergraduate student; she felt that it was "a huge time suck" and decided not to sign up for it because she did not want to "waste that much time." However, as social media has evolved, Andrea's rationale for rejecting it has changed because of what she saw as the shallow relationships that both Facebook and Twitter encouraged. For Andrea, posting random pictures of restaurants and food did not substitute for friendship and she thought that it was important for people to put more effort into their relationships:

> I liked the idea that if you and I were going to maintain a relationship, I was going to have to put effort in and you would have to put effort in and we both knew that and that was somehow reinforcement that the connection was important to both of us. I liked that idea and with Facebook it kind of undoes all of that. There's no effort required to maintain a friendship. I was just uncomfortable with that.

More recently, Andrea has become increasingly concerned about the amount of personal information available through social media and she said that her decision not to engage with social media has helped her retain control over access to her private information. Like several other interviewees, Andrea spoke about her rejection of social media as her way of asserting independence over digital technology in order to develop her identity as an independent thinker. She understood that her rejection of social media could potentially result in negative ramifications for her career, but she maintained that as an individual it was important for her to "create and manage her personal image and identity."

However, a few interviewees who have never used social media said that they felt that opting out of social media had cast a "negative stigma" over them with some friends and potential employers. Jerry, a 32-year-old electrician from Billings, did not use social media because he felt it was a waste of his time. However, Jerry said:

> Lots of people tell me, "I can't believe you're not on Facebook – I think you'd love it," – like it's just something I haven't gotten around to doing yet. I've had prospective employers ask me what I'm trying to hide when I tell them I'm not on social media. I don't think employers should have access to workers' private lives so I think it helps that I don't use social media because I know I wouldn't give a potential employer access to my Facebook or Twitter account.

Jerry also said that on occasion his social plans have been limited because he was not on social media: "Sometimes I've been left out of dinners and parties because the invites were only posted on Twitter or Facebook but it's OK because my real friends always email me or text me about their plans."

Security concerns about the misuse of her private information were the main reason Mimi, a 31-year-old waitress from Baltimore, Maryland, did not engage with social media. Yet, Mimi also mentioned getting pushback from some people when they learned that she did not engage with social media:

> When I was looking for a job, one of the restaurant managers I interviewed with gave me the stink eye when I said I wasn't on Twitter or Facebook. So, I asked him what's the problem and he told me that they liked their employees to tweet restaurant specials to their friends or post them on Facebook. I said that I'd be happy to text my friends about their specials but that I wasn't about to join Facebook or Twitter just to advertise their restaurant. He didn't look too happy about that and I wasn't surprised that I didn't get the job. And some of my friends think I'm odd because I'm not on Instagram or Twitter. A few have told me it looks sketchy and that people will think I'm hiding something. But I like that it makes me different. It's who I am and it's important to me.

8   The status of opting out

This book has showcased Raymond Williams' understanding of the role of human agency in the development and use of digital technologies. Rather than seeing individuals who did not engage with new media as unfortunate have-nots, who were being left behind in contemporary society, or as media resisters who fought social oppression created by digital technologies, or even as shortsighted individuals who committed "digital suicide" by opting out, this book took a more open and less judgmental approach by focusing directly on people's intentions and the reasons how and why they engaged with or rejected digital technologies.

Apart from a consistent preference to read paper books, this research provided little consensus about the rationale for opting out. Instead, this book illustrated the nuanced thinking and numerous reasons why people chose to use some new technologies and rejected others. Some interviewees opted out of digital technologies because of their ethical, political, environmental, religious or cultural beliefs. Other people considered new media superficial diversions that did not meet their expectations, needs or interests and by opting out they felt their time was better served focusing on other priorities. Some citizens worried about issues of privacy and security and they rejected digital technologies because they were fearful about their safety, while others constructed their cultural identities through the choices they made about their use of new media.

In many cases, the use or nonuse of digital technologies offered specific representations of how people asserted their independence, authority and agency over new media. In addition to creating one's cultural identity through their dominance over technology, in some cases the choices that people made about new technologies also illustrated how their views about digital media might be considered a type of status symbol. In other words, some people choose to opt out of digital technologies because they had the socioeconomic or cultural capital to do so.

Specifically, this concluding chapter reinforces an understanding of the role of human agency in the development and use of new technologies. It begins with a discussion of how some people use opting out as a status symbol and a way of solidifying their personal identities as independent thinkers. This chapter also focuses on ways interviewees construct their cultural identities as they assert their dominance over technology and offers some concluding remarks about the growing opting out trend.

Technology and power relations

Some people opt out of digital technologies because they have the power, status, social capital and/or the money to do so. These individuals do not need to use digital media for their livelihoods so they are able to choose which technologies if any that they wish to engage with. If necessary, they can hire other people to communicate their policies, opinions, needs and desires to others in any format necessary. As Hesselberth (2018) explains, consciously choosing to opt out of digital technologies "must be considered as an indicator of class, educational, and/or gender privilege: (as if) only the rich can disconnect and only intellectuals and leftists want to" (p. 6).

Interestingly, this is a strategy that U.S. politicians have used quite effectively during the last several years. In a 2006 speech on net neutrality, the late Senator Ted Stevens infamously described the Internet as "a series of tubes." At the time, Stevens was ridiculed for his description, because he chaired the Senate committee responsible for regulating the Internet and his depiction seemed to illustrate an extremely limited understanding of it. Since that time, some of Stevens' former colleagues have remained proud of their digital illiteracy and have continued to show little inclination to learn about or engage with new technologies. Dubbed by the press as the "Luddite Caucus," some Senators and Congress members, who currently make laws about digital technologies, do not use email, understand social media or privacy settings and they have "no idea how 21st-century technology actually works, nor any apparent motivation to learn" (Rampell 2018).

During the 2018 Congressional Hearings with Facebook, a bipartisan contingent asked Facebook CEO Mark Zuckerberg questions that suggested they did not understand how the Internet or Facebook worked. For example, Utah Senator Orin Hatch asked: "How do you sustain a business model when people don't pay for services?"; South

Carolina Senator Lindsey Graham asked: "Is Twitter the same as what you do?"; Hawaii Senator Brian Schatz asked: "If I'm emailing within WhatsApp...does that inform your advertisers?"; and Missouri Congressman Billy Long asked: "What was Facemash and is it still up and running?" (Cawley 2018). The questions the Congress members asked at the hearing have led critics to wonder how individuals who do not have a basic understanding of the digital world can craft and pass technology-related legislation.

While the current president of the U.S. has frequently said that he does not use email, in 2015, Secretary of State Hillary Clinton's use of a private email account and server became a major partisan controversy. Although Clinton said that like other officials she had used a private account and server because the U.S. government's email system was outdated and difficult to use, Republican leaders called her actions a serious and potentially criminal breach of government security. During the controversy, several politicians admitted publicly that they did not use email. Former President Bill Clinton said that he had not sent any email since he left the White House, while New York Senator Charles Schumer noted that he rarely sent email because:

> I like to communicate by talking directly to people. I find it an important part of humanity to understand not just the words that are said, but how they're said, the tone they're said in, the speed they're said with.
>
> (quoted in Parker 2015)

During the Clinton controversy, the late Arizona Senator John McCain told MSNBC's Andrea Mitchell that he had opted out of using any email because he was concerned that he might regret sending something or that his emails might be taken out of context, while Senator Graham said on NBC's "Meet the Press" that he had never in his life sent an email. In the last few years, some politicians maintained that their reluctance to use digital technologies has illustrated their "authenticity," "thoughtfulness" or "social purity." Yet, some critics have suggested that their "abstinence from email stems from not wanting to leave a paper (or digital) trail" (Rampell 2015b). Apart from concerns that Congressional leaders who were shaping new technology policy did not have a basic understanding of digital media because they were not using those technologies, politicians' rejection of email and other digital technologies has also been seen as "the ultimate status symbol – second only to sending someone to fetch your lunch" (Parker 2015).

While some Congressional leaders still do not personally send emails, engage with social media or any other digital technologies, members of their staff are often assigned to handle office email and maintain a website and social media accounts.

More than 20 of the people I interviewed said that they did not use email, yet none of them explicitly viewed their rejection of email as a status symbol. Nor did any other interviewees see their nonuse of digital technologies as a status symbol. Interestingly, none of the people who opted out of email or any other new media said they were required to use digital technologies by their employers or for their careers.

Two non-email users, both small business owners, said that they employed assistants to help them with their paperwork and that their assistants occasionally sent emails to suppliers or clients, but both said that they preferred to communicate with their clients, suppliers and employees in person or on the phone. As George, a farmer from Northern California, explained:

> I pride myself on customer service and I think the best way to run a sustainable business is to meet with my customers and suppliers directly. I think email is impersonal so I don't like to use it for my personal life or my business but my assistant sometimes uses it to connect with suppliers. I spend a lot of time visiting my customers and making sure that we're meeting their needs. And when I can't be there they know they can always reach me on the phone.

Class issues and technology

In addition to politicians asserting their class position or status by opting out of digital media, recent concerns about the impact of screens on children may be leading to a new class-based digital divide in which affluent parents are the ones who are choosing to opt out. As I discussed in Chapter 1, conceptions of the digital divide were initially based on the assumption that access to digital technologies was integral to success in contemporary democratic societies. However, in the last few years, a growing number of the economic and cultural elite have been making choices to limit their family's digital technology use. This strategy has led some parents, religious leaders, politicians, physicians and technology executives to express their concerns that "the children of poorer and middle-class parents will be raised by screens, while the children of Silicon Valley's elite will be going back to wooden toys and the luxury of human interaction" (Bowles 2018d).

In affluent communities, screen-free, play-based private preschools are currently in demand, while state-funded, online-only public pre-schools are being developed for low- and middle-income families in states like Utah, Wyoming and Montana. According to a recent study by Common Sense Media, lower income teenagers spend at least two hours longer on screens each day accessing entertainment than higher-income teenagers. In addition, researchers have found that poor and minority children are currently exposed to screens up to 50 percent more each day than affluent white children (Bowles 2018d).

In the global high-technology hub of Silicon Valley, some parents report that they are panicking about the influence of digital technologies on their children. Technology-savvy parents are not only limiting their children's screen times, but some have become so fearful about the influence of new media that they believe that its best for them to totally restrict their children's access to smartphones, computers, tablets and televisions. Some technology developers currently require their children's nannies to enforce a ban on all screen time, even going so far as to ask their nannies to sign "no-phone use contracts" in order to enforce a "zero unauthorized screen exposure" policy for their children (Bowles 2018e). But this is not only a Silicon Valley phenomenon. Affluent and middle-class parents throughout the U.S. are increasingly concerned about the influence of screens on their children's concentration and social interactions and they have been limiting their children's exposure and access to digital technologies. Rather than buying their children tablets, electronic games and other digital toys, these parents are choosing board games, microscopes, blocks, costumes and other toys that encourage their children engage in creative play and to build and explore their environment.

Several of the parents I interviewed were concerned about the in-fluence of digital technologies on their families; and as I discussed in Chapter 2, they were attempting to balance their children's screen time with sports, outdoor activities, family outings and vacations, arts and crafts and hands-on toys. Two of the people I interviewed, Angela and Ian, described themselves as "Silicon Valley parents" because they worked in the technology sector in Northern California. Both were aware that technology leaders like Steve Jobs and Bill Gates had limited their own children's screen time and they said that they were trying to do the same with their own children.

Angela, a 42-year-old programmer from Oakland, California, said that she and her husband restricted their children's use of digital technologies because "we know how over-stimulating and addictive" they can be.

Early in our relationship we saw some of our friends' kids act like zombies. They had no manners and couldn't talk with anyone and didn't seem to have any interests besides playing video games and that kind of terrified us. We made a pact that if we had children we would do our best to balance our kids' technology use so they would have a more normal childhood.

Angela has a 13-year-old son and an 11-year-old daughter, who she said participate in a variety of afterschool activities:

They're pretty scheduled. In addition to getting together with their friends, my son is in a youth soccer league and is taking trumpet lessons and my daughter is on a local swim team and is taking gymnastics lessons and learning to paint. We also have a tutor who is teaching them Mandarin and helps them with their math and science homework.

Angela said that neither of her children has a cell phone yet, but that they are able to use the family computer for their homework.

We don't really restrict their screen time but we try and keep them so busy with other activities that they don't have much time to be online. On the weekends we get out and have fun. We do family stuff like go for hikes, play at the beach, fly kites, or visit a museum or the aquarium.

Similarly, Ian, a 37-year-old technology designer from the Bay area, has two daughters who are five and seven years old. As a single father, Ian said he is committed to balancing his children's technology use:

I have a nanny who takes care of the girls when I'm at work. She gets them ready for school and helps them with any homework that they might have. I've asked her not to let the girls watch TV or use the computer in the afternoon so she usually takes them to the park or they play a game or do a puzzle together. After I get home from work, we all cook dinner together and I read to the girls before bed each night.

Both Angela and Ian's children attend private schools that limit their students' technology usage. According to Angela, "The day school that my children attend is screen-free. They read paper books, do lots of art projects and each classroom works on community service activities.

This year my daughter's class is reading to retirees at the local senior center." Ian said that his girls' elementary school is play-based and that the school encourages students to limit their technology use and to physically explore nature. According to Ian:

> None of the children are allowed to bring in phones and all of the students are encouraged to make things with their own hands. This semester, my older daughter is learning cursive and all of the class is writing letters to send to their family members.

Angela and Ian both hired people to help them care for their children and they admitted that having assistance has made it much easier for them to regulate their children's screen time. As Ian explained:

> I'm a good dad and my daughters are my number one priority. It's important for me to make sure that they don't get sucked into the technology trap. I'd never use TV or the Internet as a babysitter. They're not old enough to regulate their own screen time so it's important that I have someone to help me out with them when I'm at work.

While neither Angela nor Ian or other interviewees specifically connected their class status to their views of digital technology, several parents who restricted their children's technology usage were affluent enough to hire people to help them educate or entertain their children when they were not available. In addition, other parents saw their identity wrapped up in the decisions they made related to limiting their children's technology use. These interviewees consistently described themselves as parents who took their children's well-being seriously and prided themselves on overseeing each aspect of their education and training. They identified as parents first and to these parents, restricting their children's digital technology use was the right thing to do for them.

Fears of technology

Bill Clinton and James Patterson's 2018 best-selling novel, *The President is Missing*, focuses on Americans' current reliance on the Internet of Things and considers what would happen if the Internet was disabled. Exploring the worst-case scenario that underpins many individuals' fears of new technology, the political thriller details a cyberterrorism attack on the U.S., in which every device connected to the Internet has been infected with a virus that when activated would erase all software. Warning that in addition to all computers, servers and routers being erased, payroll, legal and bank records, law enforcement databases, social security and medical and tax records would also be wiped out, *The President is Missing* explains that the U.S. would descend into the dark ages and the cyberattack would not only lead to unemployment, but it would also cause an:

> enormous reduction in the availability of credit, a recession the likes of which would make your Depression in the 1930s look like a momentary hiccup....Widespread panic. A run on the banks. Looting of grocery stores. Rioting. Massive crime. The outbreak of diseases. All semblance of civil order gone.
>
> (Clinton and Patterson 2018, pp. 282–283)

Fears about the current U.S. reliance on digital technologies has pervaded many of the discussions within the digital temperance movement and framed many calls for people to opt out of digital technologies. As addressed in Chapter 3, many interviewees considered A.I. "terrifying" and they feared A.I.'s influence on their relationships, careers and on society as a whole. They also worried about the impact of a steady diet of digital technologies on their family's health and well-being. Some individuals were concerned that if people began to rely too heavily on digital technologies and then they somehow lost access to them, they would not be able to effectively manage their lives. During quite a few of my interviews, there was an underlying sense of concern about negative influences connected to our overreliance on digital screens. Just like Clinton and Patterson explored in their novel, interviewees of all ages, backgrounds and regions of the U.S. asked "what if" questions regarding their fears about what might happen to Americans if the Internet was disabled or destroyed by terrorists or a hostile foreign country.

Most of the interviewees who restricted their use of digital technologies for environmental, cultural, political, ethical and/or religious reasons (addressed in Chapter 5) felt that they would personally be fine if the Internet was at some point unavailable. Because several interviewees did not use smartphones or computers and rarely accessed the Internet, they said that they thought they would be prepared to handle an Internet outage. Some interviewees, who were members of intentional communities or practiced simple living, also said that because they limited their new media usage and they still relied on many older technologies, they could manage if the Internet of Things was disabled for an extended period of time. The views of Tiffany, a nurse from Ohio who practiced voluntary simplicity, resonated with several interviewees. As Tiffany explained:

> I have a credit card for emergencies but I usually pay cash for things I buy. I still have paper checks and can use them if needed. I also manually keep track of my checking account balance so there's no need for me to go online to check it. I live close to the hospital and can walk to work even in the winter. And if the stores are affected, I have a garden and lots of food that I've canned and stored and friends who do the same so we'll have food to eat and we'll be fine.

However, about half of the interviewees raised concerns about what might happen if the Internet was somehow destroyed. Bob, a 21-year-old student from Los Angeles, illustrated many interviewees' concerns in his comments about Americans' overreliance on the Internet of Things and his worries about what could happen if citizens were not able to get online. As Bob explained:

> Everything's automated now: banks, elevators, scanners, traffic lights, credit cards, alarms, water and power and sometimes I wonder what we'd do if the power grid went down and no one had online access – even for a day or two. I never carry any cash so I wouldn't even be able to buy anything. And imagine running out of gas or getting stuck in an elevator without a manual override system – scary.

Similarly, Margaret, a 73-year-old retiree from Montana, feared that "everything would fall apart if the Internet was destroyed." Margaret said she would be lost without her smartphone and believed that she would be unable to find her way if she had to drive without Google Maps and "even worse, I'd be terrified if I needed my family and couldn't reach them."

Convinced that smartphones, digital listening devices and other digital technologies were spying on them and tracking their movements, the majority of interviewees also expressed their concerns about intrusions into their privacy from smart devices. As I discussed in chapters 6 and 7, while most interviewees accepted a lack of privacy in the public realm, they were unwilling to give up their expectations of privacy in their private lives. In addition, interviewees who opted out of Facebook or other social media platforms said they did so because they were misusing or selling their personal information or because they had unethical business practices.

Developing cultural identity

For many interviewees, their views of digital technologies helped them to construct their own identities. As addressed in Chapter 4, some interviewees preferred to use older technologies like vinyl albums, typewriters, paper books or Polaroid cameras as a way of distinguishing themselves from others. Several interviewees considered this was a fundamental way they constructed their own identities and explained that their use of analog technologies went to the core of how they envisioned themselves and had become a significant aspect of their personal identity.

Stuart Hall has explained that the development of people's cultural identity is not stagnant, but continually changing; it is the result of evolving and sometimes contradictory identifications based on such things as class, gender, race and political orientation; it is also influenced by people's own historically based experiences. To illustrate the concept of contradictory identifications, Hall used the example of the 1991 Senate hearings for the appointment of Clarence Thomas to the U.S. Supreme Court. During the hearings, Thomas, an African American man with conservative political leanings, was accused of sexual harassment by Anita Hill, a former junior colleague of his who was also African American. The accusations caused a public scandal and polarized much of the country. While some African Americans supported Thomas on racial considerations, others were opposed to his confirmation based on sexual grounds. "Black women were divided, depending on whether their 'identities' as blacks or as women prevailed. Black men were also divided, depending on whether their sexism overrode their liberalism" (Hall 2000, p. 600). White Americans were equally divided based on their politics as well as how they identified regarding issues of sexism and racism. In addition, Hall noted that because at the time of the incident Thomas was considered a member of the judicial elite and Hill was a junior associate, issues of social class also influenced people's contradictory identities.

The notion of shifting and contradictory identities also emerged within this study of the opting out movement. It also offered a relevant response to those individuals who have suggested that because some individuals used digital technologies to announce that they had stopped using digital technologies, opted out of Twitter or Facebook or planned to participate in a digital detox, they were not serious about their decision to quit. Clearly, people have taken opting out seriously, but some may have experienced shifting views on how best to share their decisions with others. Throughout my interviews, several examples of shifting identities emerged. For example, several interviewees who were employed in the technology sector refused to use online banking because of the security risks involved, while others did not want their own children to use the products they made. In the second example, the interviewees' identity as parents clearly overrode their identity as technology developers.

In addition, decisions to mix analog and digital technologies (explored in Chapter 4) exposed a variety of conflicting identities, including writers who used computers for work purposes but chose a manual typewriter or bound paper books and fountain pens for their creative activities because these analog technologies expressed their authentic identities. In addition, several vinyl devotees said they did not interact socially with anyone other than vinyl lovers, because owning and listening to vinyl was a fundamental way they identified themselves and they did not think that they would be able to relate to non-vinyl users.

Overall, interviewees' opinions about their use and nonuse of digital technologies were thoughtful and nuanced, complicated and sometimes confusing, and they did not fit easily into one specific rationale or category as other researchers have done. For example, some parents who completely restricted their children's screen time wondered if they might be setting their children up for future problems relating to their peers. Angela clearly expressed this perspective when she stated:

> While I'm confident I'm doing the right thing insisting my children remain screen free as long as possible so that they can have a normal childhood, I still worry that because they aren't online they will somehow be left behind their friends. You know, that they won't have the necessary digital literacy necessary to fit in with their peers later like when they go to college and start their careers.

Ultimately, I found that the 105 people I interviewed were actively making decisions about their relationships with digital technologies. While they were sometimes unsure about the best way to address the myriad of new media, they refused to relinquish their control over these technologies.

Finally, Prince EA, a filmmaker, poet and spoken word artist from St. Louis, Missouri, challenges his followers to embrace their creativity and imagination and use their gifts in service to humanity.

Since 2015, his work has been viewed more than 500 million times on YouTube and Facebook. His videos encourage people to assess their personal lives and interactions with others and they challenge people to consider ways to make their lives more meaningful. Suggesting that our current reliance on digital technology has made individuals selfish and separate, Prince EA urges people not to let technologies exert power over their lives. Finding Facebook "an anti-social network," he encourages millions of viewers to put down their smartphones and opt out of social media in order to interact with others face-to-face and begin to develop a more humane and loving culture (Howes 2015). Notably, Prince EA imagines a world where people smile when their smartphone batteries are low, "because that will mean we'll be one bar closer to humanity" (2016). While Prince EA is not the only celebrity who is encouraging people to take control of their technology use, his message certainly resonated with many of my interviewees and people in the digital temperance movement, reminding us that we have control over digital technology and that when necessary, unplugging may just be the best alternative.

References

Adams, R.L, 2017, January 10, '10 Powerful Examples of AI in Use Today,' *Forbes.* Available from: www.forbes.com/sites/robertadams/2017/01/10/10-powerful-examples-of-artificial-intelligence-in-use-today/#28da1f72420d

American Psychological Association, 2017, February 23, 'Stress in America: Coping with Change.' *Stress in America Survey.* Available from: http://stressinamerica.org

Anderson, M, Perrin, A, and Jiang, J, 2018, '11% of Americans Don't use the Internet. Who Are They?' *Pew Research Center.* Available from: https://pewrsr.ch/20jdzst

Andriakos, J, 2017, June, 'Do a Digital Detox,' *Health.com*, p. 22.

'A Short History of Vinyl Records,' 2018, Vinyland. Available from: www.vinyland.com/index.php?main_page=vinyl&language=en

Ballentine, C, 2018, July 14, 'Could You Make it Through Dinner Without Checking Your Phone?' *The New York Times.* Available from: https://nytimes.com/2018/07/14/technology/dinner-without-cellphone.html?login-email&auth-login-email

Bartlett, J, 2018, March 4, 'Will 2018 Be the Year of the Neo-luddite?' *The Guardian.* Available from: www.theguardian.com/technology/2018/mar/04/will-2018-be-the-year-of-the-neo-luddite

Bartlett, J, 2015, March 3, 'Local Faith Leaders Reflect on National Day of Unplugging,' *San Jose Mercury News.* p. 3.

Bartmanski, D, and Woodward, I, 2015, 'The Vinyl: The Analogue Medium in the Age of Digital Reproduction,' *Journal of Consumer Culture*, vol. 15, no. 1, pp. 3–27.

Bauerlein, M, and Jeffery, C, 2018, December 4, 'It's the End of News as We Know It (and Facebook is Feeling Fine),' *Mother Jones.* Available from: www.motherjones.com/media/2018/12/facebook-propaganda-trump/?utm_source=Daily+Lab+email+list&utm_campaign=b312a90c28-daily labemail3&utm_medium=email&utm_term=0_d68264fd5e-b312a90c28-395847749&utm_source=Facebook+out+--+final+12%2F30%2F18&utm_campaign=Facebook+out+--+final+12%2F30%2F18&utm_medium=email

Bellini, J, 2018, September 20, 'Artificial Intelligence: The Robots Are Now Hiring,' *Wall Street Journal.* Available from: www.wsj.com/articles/artificial-intelligence-the-robots-are-now-hiring-moving-upstream-1537435820

Bilton, N, 2014a, July 16, 'Reclaiming Our (Real) Lives from Social Media,' *The New York Times*. Available from: www.nytimes.com/2014/07/17/fashion/reclaiming-our-rea-lives-f...

Bilton, N, 2014b, July 30, 'Digital Divide on the Wedding Aisle,' *The New York Times*. Available from: www.nytimes.com/2014/07/31/fashion/digital-weddings-2-0-hashtags-and-retweets.html?emc=etal

Bilton, N, 2013, May 13, 'Even the Tech Elites Leave Gadgets Behind,' *The New York Times*. Available from: http://bits/blogs.nytimes.com/2013/05/12/disruptions-even-the-tech-elites-leave-gadgets-behind/

Bobkowski, P, and Smith, J, 2013, 'Social Media Divide: Characteristics of Emerging Adults Who Do Not Use Social Network Websites,' *Media, Culture & Society*, vol. 35, no. 6, pp. 771–781.

'Book Publisher Revenue Up 6.2% in First Quarter of 2018,' 2018, May 25, Association of American Publishers. Available from: http://newsroom.publishers.org/book-publisher-revenue-up62-in-first-quarter-of-2018/

Borchers, C, 2015, January 15, 'Need to Unplug? There's an App for That,' *The Boston Globe*. Available from: www.bostonglobe.com/business/2015/01/12/need-unplug-there-app-for-that/

Bowles, N, 2018a, February 4, 'Early Facebook and Google Employees Form Coalition to Fight What They Built,' *The New York Times*. Available from: www.nytimes.cm/2018/02/04/technology/early-facebook-google-employees-fight-tech-html

Bowles, N, 2018b, October 26, 'A Dark Consensus About Screens and Kids Begins to Emerge in Silicon Valley,' *The New York Times*. Available from: www.nytimes.com/2018/10/26/style/phones-children-silicon-valley.html

Bowles, N, 2018c, March 23, 'Elon Musk Joins #DeleteFacebook with a Barrage of Tweets,' *The New York Times*. Available from: www.nytimes.com/2018/03/23/technology/elon-musk-deletefacebook.html

Bowles, N, 2018d, October 26, 'The Digital Gap Between Rich and Poor Kids is Not What We Expected,' *The New York Times*. Available from: www.nytimes.com/2018/10/26/style/digital-divide-screens-schools.html

Bowles, N, 2018e, October 26, 'Silicon Valley Nannies are Phone Police for Kids,' *The New York Times*. Available from: www.nytimes.com/2018/10/26/style/silicon-valley-nannies.html

Boyd, J, 2018, February 5, 'The History of Facebook: From BASIC to Global Giant,' *Brand Watch*. Available from: www.brandwatch.com/blog/history-of-facebook/

Boyle, M, 2016, December 19, 'Life Without Technology,' *The Guardian*. Available from: https://theguardian.com/commentisfree/2016/dec/19/life-without-technology-rejecting-technology

Brennen, J.S, Howard, P.N, and Nielsen, R.R, 2018, December, 'An Industry-Led Debate: How U.K. Media Cover Artificial Intelligence,' pp. 1–10. *Reuters Institute for the Study of Journalism*, Oxford.

Brooker, K, 2018, July 1, '"I was Devastated": Tim Berners-Lee, the Man Who Created the World Wide Web, Has Some Regrets,' *Vanity Fair*. Available from: www.vanityfair.com/news/2018/07/the-man-who-created-the-world-wide-web-has-some-regrets

Brynjolfsson, E, and McAfee, A, 2014, *The Second Machine Age.* New York, NY: Norton.

Burnette, M, 2018, February 13, 'Is Online Banking Safe? How to Boost Your Banking Security,' *Nerdwallet.* Available from: www.nerdwallet.com/blog/banking/online-banking-security/

Cattel, J, 2015, June 30, 'This Woman Unplugs Every Saturday (and Will Convince You to Do the Same),' *Greatist.* Available from: https://greatist.com/connect/tiffany-shlain-technology-shabbat

Caulfield, K, 2018, January 3, 'U.S. Vinyl Album Sales Hit Nielsen Music-Era Record High in 2017,' *Billboard.* Available from: www.billboard.com/articles/columns/chart-beat/8085951/us-vinyl-album-

Cawley, C, 2018, October 15, 'Politicians are Too Out of Touch to Make Laws About Tech,' *Tech.co.* Available from: https://tech.co/news/politicians-out-of-touch-laws-regulate-tech-2018-10

Chen, B, 2018, July 11, 'I Used Apple's New Controls to Limit a Teenager's iPhone Time (and It Worked!),' *The New York Times.* Available from: www.nytimes.com/2018/07/11/technology/personaltech/apple-iphone-screen-time-html

Chokshi, N, 2018, May 25, 'Is Alexa Listening? Amazon Echo Sent Out Recording of Couple's Conversation,' *The New York Times.* Available from: https://mobile.nytimes.com/2018/05/25/business/amazon-alexa-conve...echo.html?emc=edit_th_180526ni=todaysheadlines&nlid=657665000526

Clark, K, 2015, January 13, 'Zuckerburg's Sister Encourages Unplugging,' *Chronicle-Independent.* Available from: www.chronicle-independent.com/archives/35181/

Clinton, B, and Patterson, J, 2018. *The President is Missing.* New York, NY: Little, Brown.

Cooper, A, 2017, April 9, 'What is "Brainhacking"? Tech Insiders on Why You Should Care,' *60 Minutes* transcript. Available from: www.cbsnews.com/news/brain-hacking-tech-insiders-60-minutes/

Cooper, T, 2006, 'Of Scripts and Scriptures: Why Plain People Perpetuate a Media Fast?' *The Journal of American Culture*, vol. 29, no. 2, pp. 139–153.

Dance, G, LaForgia, M, and Confessore, N, 2018, December 18, 'As Facebook Raised a Privacy Wall, It Carved an Opening for Tech Giants,' *The New York Times.* Available from: www.nytimes.com/2018/12/18/technology/facebook-privacy.html?smid=nytcore-ios-share

DaPonte, J, 2018, 'Your Television is Watching You,' Index on Censorship.org, vol. 45, no. 1, pp. 88–90.

Davis, M, 2018, December 3, 'Cutting Social Media Use to 30 Mins Per Day Significantly Reduces Depression and Loneliness,' *The Big Think.* Available from: https://bigthink.com/mind-brain/social-media-causes-depression-loneliness

Dindar, M, and Akbulut, Y, 2014, 'Why Do Pre-Service Teachers Quit Facebook? An Investigation on "Quitters Forever" and "Quitters for a While,"' *Computers in Human Behavior*, vol. 39, pp. 170–176.

Douthat, R, 2017, March 11, 'Resist the Internet,' *New York Times*. Available from: www.nytimes.com/2017/03/11/opinion/sunday/resist-the-internet. html?smprod=nytcore-iphone&smid=nytcore-iphone-share

Dowd, M, 2017, 'Elon Musk's Billion-Dollar Crusade to Stop the A.I. Apocalypse,' *Vanity Fair Magazine*. Available from: www.vanityfair.com/news/2017/03/elon-musk-billion-dollar-crusade-to-stop-ai-space-x

Dredge, S, 2018, January 27, 'Mobile Phone Addiction? It's Time to Take Back Control,' *The Guardian*. Available from: www.theguardian.com/technology/2018/jan/27/mobile-phone-addiction-apps-break-the-habit-take-back-control

Ediriwira, A, 2016, July 22, 'The 8 Best Vinyl Subscription Services to Grow Your Record Collection,' *The VinylFactory.com*. Available From: https://thevinylfactory.com/features/the-8-best-vinyl-subscription-services-to-help-grow-your-record-collection/

Edwards, H.S, 2017a, May 15, 'Alexa Takes the Stand: Listening Devices Raise Privacy Issues,' *Time*, vol. 189, no. 18, pp. 28–29.

Edwards, H, 2017b, 'Facebook is the Big Tech Company that People Trust Least,' *Quartz.com*. Available from: https://qz.com/1085588/survey-facebook-is-the-big-tech-company-that-people-trust-least/

Eisenstein, E, 1997, 'From the Printed Word to the Moving Image,' *Social Research*, vol. 64, no. 3, pp. 1049–1066.

Foot, K, 2014, 'The Online Emergence of Pushback on Social Media in the United States: A Historical Discourse Analysis,' *International Journal of Communication*, vol. 8, pp. 1313–1342.

Fowler, G, 2018a, January 25, 'App Aims to Curb Phone Addiction,' *Times Herald*, p. 9.

Fowler, G, 2018b, October 18, 'I Fell for Facebook Fake News. Here's Why Millions of You Did Too,' *The Washington Post*. Available from: www.washingtonpost.com/technology/2018/10/18/i-fell-facebook-fake-news-heres-why-millions-you-did-too/?utm_term=.7c282958e9d9&wpisrc=nl_most&wpmm=1

Friedman, D, 2018, April, 'Do you Need a Digital Detox?' *Health.com*, pp. 102–105.

Garimella, K, 2018, August 7, 'Job Loss from A.I.? There's More to Fear,' *Forbes*. Available from: www.forbes.com/sites/cognitiveworld/2018/08/07/job-loss-from-ai-theres-more-to-fear/#5adb812423eb

Garside, J, 2015, May 25, 'Philip Zimmermann: King of Encryption Reveals His Fears for Privacy,' *The Guardian*. Available from: www.theguardian.com/technology/2015/may/25/philip-zimmermann-king-encryption-reveals-fears-privacy?CMP=share_btn_link

George, A, 2011, 'Luddite and Proud,' *New Scientist*, vol. 212, no. 2844/2845, pp. 40–41.

Gleiberman, O, 2017, August 17, 'Film Review: "California Typewriter,"' *Variety.com*. Available from: https://variety.com/2017/film/reviews/california-typewriter-review-tom-hanks-1202531511/

Greene, D, 2017, October 16, 'Tom Hanks is Obsessed with Typewriters (So he Wrote a Book About Them),' *NPR*. Available from: www.npr.org/2017/10/16/557636219/tom-hanks-is-obsessed-with-typewriters-so-he-wrote-a-book-about-them

Griffin, A, 2014, December 2, 'Stephen Hawking: AI Could Be the End of Humanity,' *The Independent*. Available from: www.independent.co.uk/news/science/stephen-hawking-ai-could-be-the-end-of-humanity-9898320.html

Grossman, L, 2015, June 1, 'Good Tech Gone Bad,' *TIME*, pp. 51–53.

Grothaus, M, 2018, December 13, 'How Our Data Got Hacked, Scandalized, and Abused in 2018,' *Fast Company*. Available from: www.fastcompany.com/90272858/how-our-data-got-hacked-scandalized-and-abused-in-2018

Gunkel, D.J, 2003, 'Second Thoughts: Toward a Critique of the Digital Divide,' *New Media & Society*, vol. 5, no. 4, pp. 499–522.

Haas, P, 2017, December 15, 'The Real Reason to Be Afraid of Artificial Intelligence,' *Ted Talks*. Available from: www.youtube.com/watch?v=TRzBk_KuIaM&t=163s

Haber, M, 2013, July 4, 'A Trip to Camp to Break a Tech Addition,' *The New York Times*. Available from: www.nytimes.com/2013/07/07/fashion/a-trip-to-camp-to-break-a-tech-addiction.html

Haberman, M, 2018, July 20, 'Maggie Haberman: Why I Needed to Pull Back from Twitter,' Sunday Review, *The New York Times*. Available from: www.mnytimes.com/2018/07/20/sunday-review/maggie-haberman-twitter-donald-trump.html

Hall, S, 2000, 'The Question of Cultural Identity,' in *Modernity: An Introduction to Modern Societies*, eds. Stuart Hall, David Held, Don Hubert and Kenneth Thompson, pp. 596–632. London: Blackwell.

Harambam, J, Aupers, S, and Houtman, D, 2013, 'The Contentious Gap,' *Information, Communication & Society*, vol. 16, no. 7, pp. 1093–1114.

Helfet, G, 2018, July 9, 'Over 7.6 Million Vinyl LPs Were Sold in the US During the First Half of 2018,' *The Vinyl Factory*. Available from: https://thevinylfactory.com/news/record-vinyl-sales-usa-first-half-2018/

Hesselberth, P, 2018, 'Discourses on Disconnectivity and the Right to Disconnect,' *New Media & Society*, vol. 20, no. 5 pp. 1994–2010.

Hill, K, and Mattu, S, 2018, April, 'What Your Smart Devices Know (and Share) About You,' *Ted Talk*. Available from: www.ted.com/talks/kashmir_hill_and_surya_mattu_what_your_smart_devices_know_and_share_about_you?language=en

Hindman, D.B, 2000, 'The Rural-Urban Digital Divide,' *Journalism & Mass Communication Quarterly*, vol. 77, no. 3, pp. 549–560.

Hirsh, S, 2017, February 14, 'Ed Sheeran Doesn't Have a Cell Phone,' *Teen Vogue*. Available from: https://teenvogue.com/story/ed-sheeran-doesnt-have-cell-phone

Holley, P, 2018, August 8, 'Soon, the Most Beautiful People in the World May No Longer Be Human,' *The Washington Post*. Available from: www.wash ingtonpost.com/technology/2018/08/08/soon-most-beautiful-people-world-may-no-longer-be-human/?utm_term=.c532b763cf7

Horsey, D, 2017, March 31, 'Robots, Not Immigrants, Are Taking American Jobs,' *Los Angeles Times*. Available from: http://latimes.com/opinion/topoftheticket/la-na-tt-robots-j...=lwAR3GcugWbpyFzApLLMqsBuYh-FRXEAEbsSblmFDZDkHRTeb7OK2ytjRWxvHA

Howes, L, 2015, 'Open Your Mind and Move the World with Prince EA.' School of Greatness Podcast, Episode 202. Available from: https://lewis howes.com/podcast/prince-ea/

Irvine, M, 2012, October 29, 'Can True Solitude Be Found in a Wired World?' *Boston Globe*. Available from: www.bostonglobe.com/business/2012/10/28/can-true-solitude-be-found-in-a-wired-world?

Jiang, J, 2018, 'How Teens and Parents Navigate Screen Time and Device Distractions,' Pew Research Center. Available from: http://pew internet.org/2018/08/22/how-teens-and-parents-navigate-screen-time-and-device-distractions/

Kale, S, 2018, August 29, 'Logged Off: Meet the Teens Who Refuse to Use Social Media,' *The Guardian*. Available from: www.theguardian.com/society/2018/aug/29/teens-desert-social-media

Karppi, T, 2011, 'Digital suicide and the Biopolitics of Leaving Facebook,' *Transformations*, vol. 20, pp. 1–13.

Katz, J, and Aspden, P, 1998, *Telecommunications Policy*, vol. 22, no. 4–5, pp. 327–339.

'Killer Robots: Tech Experts Warn Against AI Arms Race,' 2015, July 29, *BBC*. Available from: www.bbc.com/news/technology-33686581

Kingsley, P, and Anderson, T, 1998, 'Facing Life Without the Internet,' *Internet Research: Electronic Networking Applications and Policy*, vol. 8, no. 4, pp. 303–312.

Kissane, A, 2018, March 2, 'Go Back to Smartphone? No Thanks, Says Ryan,' *Daily Mail*, p. 18.

Klass, P, 2018, December 17, 'The Case for Creative Play in a Digital Age,' *The New York Times*. Available from: www.nytimes.com/2018/12/17/well/family/the-case-for-creative-play-in-a-digital-age.html

Kraybill, D, 2001, *The Riddle of Amish Culture, Second Edition*. Baltimore: Johns Hopkins University Press.

Krabill, D, 1998, 'Plain Reservations: Amish and Mennonite Views of Media and Computers,' *Journal of Mass Media Ethics*, vol. 13, no. 2, pp. 99–110.

Krummenacher, V, 2012, July 1, 'If You Care About the Sound of Recorded Music, There's Nothing Better Than Vinyl,' *Wired Magazine*, vol. 20, no. 7, p. 44.

Kuntsman, A, and Miyake, E, 2016, 'Paradoxes of Digital Dis/Engagement: A Follow Up Study,' *White Rose Research*. Available from: http://eprints.whiterose.ac.uk/114828/

Kurzweil, R, 2005, *The Singularity is Near. When Humans Transcend Biology.* New York, NY: Viking Press.

Lange, D, 2017, August 7, 'Typewriters are Making a Comeback,' *Senior Planet.* Available from: https://seniorplanet.org/typewriters-are-making-a-comeback/

Langley, W, 2015, January 20, 'Old is Gold: The Appeal of a Low-Tech Lifestyle,' *Sunday Telegraph*, p. 16.

Lazenby, P, 2012, January 23, 'Rage Against the Machine,' *New Statesman*, p. 14.

Lewis-Kraus, G, 2016, December 18, 'The Great A.I. Awakening,' *New York Times Magazine.* Available from: www.nytimes.com/2016/12/14/magazine/the-great-ai-awakening.html

Liao, S.M., 2018, November 24, 'Do You Have a Moral Duty to Leave Facebook?' *The New York Times Sunday Review.* Available from: www.nytimes.com/2018/11/24/opinion/sunday/facebook-immoral.html

Livio, O, and Weinblatt, K.T., 2007, 'Discursive Legitimation of a Controversial Technology: Ultra-Orthodox Jewish Women in Israel and the Internet. *The Communication Review*, vol. 10, pp. 29–56.

Lohr, S, 2018, March 8, 'It's True: False News Spreads Faster and Wider and Humans are to Blame,' *The New York Times.* Available from: www.nytimes.com/2018/03/08/technology/twitter-fake-news-research.html

Mack, R.L., 2001, *The Digital Divide: Standing at the Intersection of Race and Technology*, Durham, NC: Carolina Academic Press.

Maheshwari, S, 2018, March 31, 'Hey, Alexa, What Can You Hear? And What Will You Do With It?' *The New York Times.* Available from: www.nytimes.com/2018/03/31/business/media/amazon-google-privacy-digital-assistants.html

Maheshwari, S, 2017, February 7, 'Is Your Vizio Television Spying on You? What to Know,' *The New York Times.* Available from: www.nytimes.com/2017/02/07/business/vizio-television-vixio-collected-viewers-habits-consent.html

Malik, N, 2018, October 4, 'We Need to Examine the Ethics and Governance of Artificial Intelligence,' *Forbes.* Available from: www.forbes.com/sites/nikitamalik/2018/10/04/we-need-to-examine-the-ethics-and-governance-of-artificial-intelligence/#2afc460b7aab

Mawad, M, and Rahn, C, 2015, January 24, 'Twitter and Tumblr Execs Ditch Smartphones to Combat Addiction,' *Daily Herald.* Available from: http://dailyherald.com/article/20150124/business/150129547/

McGregor, J, 2018, November 20, 'You've Come to Expect Your Data Is at Risk When You Shop. Don't Forget About When You're at Work,' *The Washington Post.* Available from: www.washingtonpost.com/business/2018/11/20/you've-come-exp...u-shop-dont-forget-about-when-youre-work/?utm_term=.751c10654a5f

McKnight, Z, 2016, July 5, 'Grown-ups Can Gear Up for Summer Camp,' *Toronto Star.* Available from: http://0-search.ebscohost.com.libus.csd.mu.edu/login.aspx?direct=true&db=n5h&AN=6FPTS2016070538745889&site=eds-live

Mele, C, 2017, January 12, 'Levi Felix, a Proponent of Disconnecting from Technology, Dies at 32,' *The New York Times*. Available from: www.ny times.com/2017/01/12/us/obituary-levi-felix-digital-detox.html

Miller, M, 2015, May 29, 'Ten Reasons to Still Consider a Basic Flip Phone in Today's Smartphone World,' *ZDNet*. Available from: www.zdnet.com/article/ten-reasons-to-still-consider-a-basic-flip-phone-in-todays-smartphone-world/

Miller, P, 2013, May 1, 'I'm Still Here: Back Online After a Year Without the Internet,' *The Verge*. Available from: www.theverge.com/2013/5/1/4279674/im-still-here-back-online-after-a-year-without-the-internet

Mitchell, H, 2014, April 30, 'To Attract Campers, a Promise They Will Unplug,' *Wall Street Journal*. Available from: http://online.wsj.com/articles/SB 10001424052702304677904579533371...

Morrison, S, and Gomez, R, 2014, 'Pushback: Expressions of Resistance to the "Evertime" of Constant Online Connectivity,' *First Monday*, vol. 19, no. 8, pp. 1–15.

Murthy, S, and Mani, M, 2013, 'Discerning Rejection of Technology,' *Sage Open*, April–June, vol. 3, no. 2, pp. 1–10.

Newman, N, 2018, November, 'The Future of Voice and the Implications for News,' Digital News Project, Reuters Institute for the Study of Journalism, pp. 1–45.

Oliver, J, 2018, September 23, 'Facebook: Last Week Tonight with John Oliver, HBO,' *YouTube*. Available from: www.youtube.com/watch?v=OjPYm EZxACM

Osnos, E, 2018, September 17, 'Can Mark Zuckerberg Fix Facebook Before It Breaks Democracy?' *The New Yorker*. Available from: www.new yorker.com/magazine/2018/09/17/can-mark-zuckerberg-fix-facebook-before-it-breaks-democracy

Pappalardo, J, 2018, September 18, 'Fake News is Sparking an A.I. Arms Race,' *Popular Mechanics*. Available from: www.popularmechanics.com/technology/a23286956/fake-news-ai-arms-race/

Parker, A, 2015, March 11, 'In Era of Email, Some Senators Do Just Fine Without It,' *The New York Times*, A1.

Pelaez, A.L, 2014, *The Robotics Divide*. London: Springer-Verlag.

Petrow, S, 2015, January 11, 'Desire to Unplug Resonates in New Year,' *USA Today*. Available from: www.usatoday.com/story/news/nation/2015/01/10/digital-det0x/21

Portwood-Stacer, L, 2012, 'Media Refusal and Conspicuous Non-consumption: The Performative and Political Dimensions of Facebook Abstention,' *New Media & Society*, vol. 15, no. 7, pp. 1041–1057.

PrinceEA, 2016, 'Anti-Social Network.' Available from: www.princeea.com

Purves, M, 2018, December 26, 'Let the Fountain Pens Flow!' *The New York Times*. Available from: www.nytimes.com/2018/12/26/style/fountain-pens.html

Rainie, L, 2018, '"Americans" Complicated Feelings About Social Media in an Era of Privacy Concerns,' *Pew Research Center*. Available from: www.pewresearch.org/staff/lee.rainie/

Rampell, C, 2018, August 20, 'Our Politicians Have No Idea How the Internet Works,' *The Washington Post*. Available from: www.washingtonpost.com/opinions/how-can-congress-police-the-internet-when-they-dont-even-understand-it/2018/08/20/46f6baa6-a4b4-11e8-97ce-cc9042272f07_story.html?utm_term=.ec0c295ed23a

Rampell, C, 2015a, April 10, 'The Robots and Your Job,' *The Washington Post*, p. A23.

Rampell, C, 2015b, March 13, 'Offline and Out of Touch in the Senate,' *Arca-Max Washington Post Writers Group*. Available from: www.arcamax.com/politics/mod/catherinerampell/s-1626094

Ranger, S, 2018, August 21, 'What is the IoT? Everything you Need to Know About the Internet of Things Right Now,' *ZNet*. Available from: www.zdnet.com/article/what-is-the-internet-of-things-everything-you-need-to-know-about-the-iot-right-now/

Rauch, J, 2014, 'Constructive Rituals of Demediatization: Spiritual, Corporeal and Mixed Metaphors in Popular Discourse About Unplugging.' *Explorations in Media Ecology*, vol. 13, no. 3–4, pp. 237–252.

Rice, R, and Katz, J, 2003, 'Comparing Internet and Mobile Phone Usage: Digital Divides of Usage, Adoption, and Dropouts.' *Telecommunications Policy*, vol. 27, pp. 597–623.

Richter, F, 2018, April 20, 'The Surprising Comeback of Vinyl Records,' *The Statistics Portal*. Available from: www.statista.com/chart/7699/lp-sales-in-the-united-states/

Romm, T, 2019, January 21, 'France Fines Google Nearly $57 Million for First Major Violation of New European Privacy Regime,' *The Washington Post*. Available from: www.washingtonpost.com/world/europe/france-fines-google-nearly-57-million-for-first-major-violation-of-new-european-privacy-regime/2019/01/21/89e7ee08-1d8f-11e9-a759-2b8541bbbe20_story.html?utm_term=.248b4377b03b

Romm, T, and Harwell, D, 2018, September 13, 'Facebook Ramps Up Effort to Combat Fake Images, Video,' *The Washington Post*. Available from: www.washingtonpost.com/technology/2018/09/13/facebook-ramps-up-effort-combat-fake-images-video/?utm_term=.611c82e9eb3d

Roose, K, 2018, February 10, 'His 2020 Campaign Message: The Robots are Coming,' *The New York Times*. Available from: www.nytimes.com/2018

Ross, M, 2014, September 1, 'Greetings from Tech-free Camp,' *The Boston Globe*. Available from: www.bostonglobe.com/opinion/2014/08/31/greetings-from-tech-fr

'Safeguards for Using Technology,' 2015, The Church of Jesus Christ of Latter-Day Saints. Available from: https://missionary.lds.org/content/dam/mportal/missionary/pdfs/mobile-device/safeguards-for-using-technology.pdf

Sample, I, 2018, November 5, 'Tim Berners-Lee Launches Campaign to Save the Web from Abuse,' *The Guardian*. Available from: www.theguardian.com/technology/2018/nov/05/tim-brners-lee-launches-campaign-to-save-the-web-from-abuse

Sample, I, 2016, May 20, 'A.I. will Create "Useless Class" of Human, Predicts Bestselling Historian,' *The Guardian*. Available from: www.theguardian.com/technology/2016/may/20/silicon-assassins-condemn-humans-life-useless-artificial-intelligence

Sarhan, A, 2017, December 22, 'Planned Obsolescence: Apple Is Not the Only Culprit,' *Forbes.com*. Available from: www.forbes.com/sites/adamsarhan/2017/12/22/planned-obsolescence-apple-is-not-the-0only-culprit/#30ef19e43cf2

Satariano, A, and Isaac, M, 2018, December 5, 'Facebook Used People's Data to Favor Certain Partners and Punish Rivals, Documents Show,' *The New York Times*. Available from: www.nytimes.com/2018/12/05/technology/facebook-documents-uk-parliament.html

Sax, D, 2017, November 18, 'Our Love Affair with Digital Is Over,' *The New York Times*. Available from: www.nytimes.com/2017/11/18/opinion/sunday/internet-digital-technology-return-to-analog.html

Sekula, S, 2014, December 9, 'Digital Detox: Six Unplugged Vacations Around the World,' *USA Today*. Available from: http://usatoday.com/story/travel/hotels/2014/12/09/unplugged-hotel...

Sih, D, 2014, June 27, 'Why I End Each Week with a Digital Detox,' *Lifehacker*, Australia. Available from: www.lifehacker.com.au/2014/06/why-i-end-each-week-with-a-digital-detox/

Silver, D, et al., 2017, October 19, 'Mastering the Game of Go Without Human Knowledge,' *Nature*, vol. 550, pp. 354–359. Available from: www.nature.com/articles/nature24270

The Simplicity Collective (2018), 'What Is Voluntary Simplicity?'. Available from: http://simplicitycollective.com/start-here/what-is-voluntary-simplicity-2

Singer, N, 2018, July 9, 'Facebook's Push for Facial Recognition Prompts Privacy Alarms,' *The New York Times*. Available from: www.nytimes.com/2018/07/09/technology/facebook-facial-recognition-privacy.html?smi=nytcore-ios-share

Smith, A, and Anderson, M, 2017, 'Automation in Everyday Life,' *Pew Research Center*. Available from: www.pewresearch.org

Smith, C, 2018, May 10, 'Alexa and Siri Can Hear This Hidden Command. You Can't,' *The New York Times*. Available from: www.nytimes.com/2018/05/10/technology/alexa-siri-hidden-command-audio-attacks.html

Soltan, L, 2018, 'Digital Responsibility,' *Digitalresponsibility.org*. Available from: www.digitalresponsibility.org/sad-factsp-on-techtrash

Southerden, L, 2017, April 8, 'Switch Off and Tune In,' *Sydney Morning Herald*, p. 16.

Sparks, C, 2013, 'What Is the "Digital Divide" and Why Is It Important?' *Javnost – The Public*, vol. 20, no. 2, pp. 27–46.

Stieger, S, Burger, C, Bohn, M, and Voracek, M, 2013, 'Who Commits Virtual Identity Suicide? Differences in Privacy Concerns, Internet Addiction, and Personality Between Facebook Users and Quitters,' *Cyberpsychology, Behavior, and Social Networking*, vol. 16, no. 9, pp. 629–635.

Sullivan, A, 2016, September 19, 'My Distraction Sickness – and Yours,' *New York Magazine*. Available from: http://nymag.com/selectall/2016/09/andrew-sullivan-technology

'Technology Use Policy,' 2018, Twin Tiers Christian Academy. Available from: www.twintierschristianacademy.org/technology-use-policy.html

'The 10 Largest Privacy Threats in 2018,' 2018, August 23, Infosec Institute. Available from: https://resources.infosecinstitute.com/the-10-largest-privacy-threats-in-2018/#gref

Thoren, C, Edenius, M, Eriksson-Londstrum, J, and Kitzmann, A, 2017, 'The Hipster's Dilemma: What Is Analogue or Digital in the Post-Digital Society?' *Convergence, The International Journal of Research into New Media Technologies*, pp. 1–16.

Turkle, S, 2018, August 11, 'There Will Never Be an Age of Artificial Intimacy,' *The New York Times*. Available from: www.nytimes.com/2018/08/11/opinion/there-will-never-be-an-age-of-artificial-intimacy.html

Turkle, S, 2015, September 27, 'Stop Googling. Let's Talk,' *The New York Times*, Sunday Review, p. 1, 6.

Twenge, J, 2017, September, 'Have Smartphones Destroyed a Generation?' *The Atlantic*. Available from: https://theatlantic.com/magazine/archive/2017/09/has-the-smartphone-destroyed-a-generation/534198/?utm_source=atifb

Valentino-DeVries, J, Singer, N, Keller, M, and Krolik, A., 2018, December 10, 'Your Apps Know Where You Were Last Night, and They're Not Keeping it Secret,' *The New York Times*. Available from: www.nytimes.com/interactive/2018/12/10/business/location-ata-privacy-apps.html

Vargas, E, 2017, 'Digital Addiction?' *20/20 ABC*. Available from: http://0-search.ebscohost.com.libus.csd.mu.edu/login.aspx?direct=true&db=bwh&AN=123647223&site=eds-live

Victor, D, 2016, September 2, 'No the Internet Has Not Killed the Printed Book. Most People Still Prefer Them,' *The New York Times*. Available from: www.nytimes.com/2016/09/03/business/no-the-internet-has-not-killed-the-printed-book-most-people-still-prefer-them/

Weaver, N, 2018, June 16, '25 Celebrities who Refuse to Use Social Media,' *America's Spotlight*. Available from: https://americasspotlight.com/entertainment/25-celebrities-who-refuse-to-use-social-media.html/

Weise, K, 2018, September 20, 'Hey, Alexa, Why Is Amazon Making a Microwave?' *The New York Times*. Available from: www.nytimes.com/2018/09/20/technology/amazon-alexa-new-features-proucts.html

Weissmann, J, 2018, October 10, 'Amazon Created a Hiring Tool Using A.I. It Immediately Started Discriminating Against Women,' *Slate*. Available from: https://slate.com/business/2018/10/amazon-artificial-intelligence-hiring-discrimination-women.html

Weller, C, 2018, January 14, 'Bill Gates Is Surprisingly Strict About his Kids' Tech Use – and It Should be a Red Flag for the Rest of Us,' *Business Insider*. Available from: www.businessinsider.com/how-bill-gates-limits-tech-use-for-his-kids-2018-1

Whitney, L, 2018, October, 'How They Track You,' *AARP Bulletin*, pp. 36–38.

Williams, A, 2008, August 31, 'Another Spin for Vinyl,' *The New York Times*, section ST, p. 1.

Williams, R, 1974/1992, *Television: Technology and Cultural Form*, Hanover: Wesleyan University Press.

Williams, R, 1977/1988, *Marxism and Literature.* Oxford: Oxford University Press.

Woodstock, L, 2014, 'Media Resistance: Opportunities for Practice Theory and New Media Research,' *International Journal of Communication*, vol. 8, pp. 1983–2001.

'World's First AI News Anchor Unveiled in China,' 2018, November 9, *The Guardian*. Available from: www.theguardian.com/world/2018/nov/09/worlds-first-ai-news-anchor-unveiled-in-china

Wyatt, S, 2003, 'Non-Users Also Matter: The Construction of Users and Non-Users of the Internet,' in *How Users Matter: The Co-Construction of Users and Technology*, ed. Nelly Oudshoorn and Trevor Pinch, pp. 67–79. Cambridge, MA: MIT Press.

Wyatt, S, Thomas, G, and Terranova, T, 2002, 'They Came, They Surfed, They Went Back to the Beach,' in *Conceptualizing Use and Non-Use of the Internet,' Virtual Society? Technology, Cyberbole, Reality*, ed. Steve Woolgar, pp. 23–40. Oxford, UK: Oxford University Press.

Yeshiva Elementary School Parent Handbook, 2013, September, 5115 West Keefe Ave., Milwaukee, WI 53216, pp. 1–10.

Yochim, C, and Biddinger, M, 2005, 'It Kind of Gives You that Vintage Feel: Vinyl Records and the Trope of Death,' International Communication Association Conference Papers, pp. 1–28. Communication Source, EBSCOhost.

Index

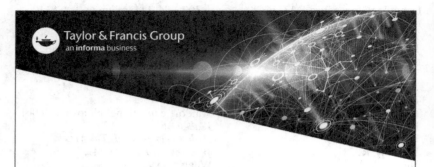

9781032338361